51 1/2 Shades of Brown

The Not-So-Perfect Tales of a Picture-Perfect Marriage

Wayne & Laura Brown

Copyright © 2018 by Wayne & Laura Brown

All rights reserved. This book or any portion thereof may not be reproduced or used in any manner whatsoever without the express written permission of the publisher except for the use of brief quotations in a book review.

Although the author and publisher have made every effort to ensure the information in this book was correct at press time, the author and publisher do not assume and hereby disclaim any liability to any party for any loss, damage, or disruption caused by errors or omissions.

We have tried to recreate events, locales, and conversations from our memories of them. Some names and identifying details were changed to protect the privacy of individuals. We may have changed some identifying characteristics and details such as physical properties, occupations, and places of residence.

Unless indicated otherwise, all scripture is from the NEW AMERICAN STANDARD BIBLE®, Copyright © 1960, 1962, 1963, 1968, 1971, 1972, 1973, 1975, 1977, 1995, by The Lockman Foundation. Used by permission."

Editing by Anna K. Brenner - anna4freelance@gmail.com

When possible, we used locally sourced talent for our publishing needs.
Meet our Chattanooga Design Team!

Cover design by MS Designs -www.msdesignandphotography.com

Back Cover:

- Author photograph by Hacker Media - www.hackermedias.com
- Hair by Kim Craig – Kim's Natural Hair Studio – kimcraig2011@gmail.com
- Makeup – Tia Taylor-Clark - Janeoftradesupscaleresale@gmail.com
- Laura's Shoes – Customized by Reena Davis – reenaoncourse@yahoo.com

Printed in the United States of America

First Printing, 2018

ISBN 978-1-941749-77-7

Library of Congress Control Number 2018905936

 4-P Publishing

Chattanooga, TN 37411

Make the Connection

 Facebook www.facebook.com/51andahalfshades

 Laura - www.coachlaurabrown.com

E-mail- coachlaurabrown@swatbookcamp.com

 Wayne -www.bridgenthegap.com

E-mail – wayne@bridgenthegap.com

* Please consider leaving us a review on Amazon!

Coloring Book & Prayer Journal
Also Available

Go to www.coachlaurabrown.com and subscribe to our mailing list to download a **FREE** sample!

Workshops & Coaching Events

Picture-Perfect Power Couple Marriage Encounter

A two-day event designed to empower couples with creative strategies to cultivate a satisfying and productive marriage

Dream Team – Power Couples Unite!
- o Discover Your Purpose
- o Develop Personality Synergy
- o Learn Your Lead Language

Picture This – The Power of a Vision-Driven Marriage
- o Discover Your Marital Purpose
- o Develop Your Marriage Vision Statement
- o Design Your Vision Canvas

The Art of War - Handle Conflict with P.O.I.S.E. & C.A.L.M.
- o Practice Communication Etiquette
- o Discover D.A.M. Barriers to Listening
- o Master the F'ing Weapons of War

Get S.H.I.F.T. Done – The Power Couple System for Success
- o Develop a Plan for Your Next Power Move
- o Create S.U.P.E.R. S.M.A.R.T. Goals
- o Design Your Next Level

*Ask about the virtual Picture-Perfect Marriage Encounter

Dedication

To our granddaughters, Serenity and Harmony, thank you for adding your beautiful shades of color to our lives. We love you both.

In memory of our grandson, Justice, your time in our lives was brief, but your smile will color our memories for a lifetime.
May 5th, 2012 – October 15th, 2012

Acknowledgments

There were many moving pieces to complete this book. We thank our children, Ouidaintria, Aurelius, and LaTasha, for agreeing to let us share their not so perfect moments in life. You three have taught us valuable lessons about life, love, sacrifice, and power of forgiveness.

Thanks to our beta readers, Christopher, Kathy, Rich, and Monica. Your early inputs helped shape our content.

A big thanks to ALL our family and friends along the way, especially Ed, who gracefully declined to dance with me on that fateful night.

We thank our Facebook friends for encouraging us to write this book. Who knew all those thumbs up would turn into a book?

Last, but certainly not least, we thank God, who, in His divine wisdom, saw past our faults and failures and brought us together to create this beautiful (in our eyes) masterpiece marriage.

Table of Contents

Foreword 15
Introduction 17
Beale AFB, California 1990-1994 19

  1 Short-Sighted 20
  2 No Parking on the Dance Floor 27
  3 Who Let the Dogs Out? 30
  4 Things You Learn in the Backseat 33
  5 Three's Company— Six is Wild 37
  6 Hidden in Plain Sight 44
  7 The Writing on the Wall 47
  8 Check Your Bags at the Door 50
  9 Exes and Ohs! 53
  10 Shut the Front Door 56
  11 Rain Dance Romance 62
  12 The Run Around 65
  13 Waterbed Rumble 68
  14 Proposal Gone Wrong 71
  15 Busted Knuckles 74
  16 Runaway Bride 76
  17 Graveyard Gratitude 79
  18 Non-fatal Attraction 82
  19 Man Down, Thumbs Up 85

20	Indecent Proposal	89
21	A Man is Just Gonna be a Man	92
22	Don't Ask, Don't Tell?	94
23	The Silence of the Fam	98

Ramstein Air Base, Germany 1994-1998 103

24	Burnt Cookies & Scorched Feelings	104
25	Soul Matters	117
26	Speedo Man	119
27	Downhill Screams	122
28	Uphill Battles	125
29	The Hole on My Butt	128
30	The "BUT" in Our Lives	131

Seymour Johnson AFB, NC 1998-2005 135

31	Time-Share Take Down	136
32	Internet Mojo	139
33	Sex-ish - The Naked Truth	142
34	Running Stop Signs	147
35	Broke Down in Kentucky	150
36	Missed the Bus	154
37	The Napkin of Doom	157
38	Mr. Telephone Man	164
39	Sleeping with the Enemy	166
40	Soul Mates	171

Hill AFB, Utah 2005-2009 ... 177

    41 Keep it All Together ... 178

    42 No Blanket Blues ... 182

    43 Can't We All Just Get Along? ... 184

    44 No Time for Tears ... 186

    45 The Kansas Epiphany ... 189

Chattanooga, TN 2009 –Present ... 193

    46 It Has Good Bones ... 194

    47 Big Shoes & Seasoned Words ... 198

    48 The Longest Ride ... 200

    49 Dutch Oven Casket ... 204

    50 Great Balls of Fire ... 207

    51 Dream Team ... 208

    $51^{1/2}$ The 1/2 Has Not Been Told ... 213

The Sum of All Shades ... 215

    Meet Wayne and Laura ... 219

    Workshops & Coaching Events ... 221

Foreword

Witty, informative, sober, and educational, *51 ½ Shades of Brown* serves well as a transparent compilation "bible" of survival in the areas of marriage, family, and parenting. An anthem for "togetherness," this book reflects how beautiful marriage can be. It can be a one of a kind artwork, a masterpiece made up of what at times can be indifference coupled with flaws, love, honor, and respect; this work includes the essential ingredients for a marriage that can and will endure!

Having known Wayne and Laura since 1998, I have always thoroughly enjoyed their "his and her" take on the intricate beauty of marriage. Full of detail, humor, and victory, *51 ½ Shades of Brown* expertly demonstrates Wayne and Laura's power of commitment, laughter, fun, and longsuffering. This book gives the reader hope in the bond, sanctity, and covenant of marriage, further epitomizing the authors' words, "A seasoned word, in the kairos moment, can be life-changing."

Dr. Miranda Y. Pearson
Licensed Professional Mental Health, Behavioral Health, and Substance Abuse Counselor

As a relationship specialist, I have had the privilege of working with couples for well over twenty years. I have witnessed the challenges couples face today in their relationships.

Couples often assume you must have a perfect beginning to have a satisfying and fulfilled marriage.

Wayne and Laura skillfully express in this book that all the pieces of the puzzle do not have to fit perfectly in the beginning. It takes time, a willingness to learn, and commitment to work together.

I admire the way Wayne and Laura have sprinkled their anecdotes with humor and life lessons that are not only relatable but also applicable.

This book will take you on a journey of their marriage and give you a snapshot of their lives. As you are drawn into their lives, you will also be challenged to look at your own marriage and pick up the tools offered to you to create and cultivate your own colorful "shades" of marriage.

David Banks, Ph.D.
Certified Relationship Specialist
Relationship Coach

Introduction

What words or images come to mind when you think of marriage? Is it love, romance, stress, anger, failure, happiness, friendship, or something else? The correct answer is all the above. Marriages are unique. All marriages will reflect the hearts of the two people involved in it.

Our story is about two flawed people with flawed circumstances who came together to create an extraordinary marriage masterpiece. Some people may prefer a romanticized fairytale. Wayne and I can't offer you a fairytale. But we are here to encourage you to get past the fairytale desire for princes on white horses and princesses in need of rescue. Instead, seek the kind of person you can make history with for a lifetime! That is more satisfying than a fairytale.

Our friends and family often comment on the wonderful marriage we *seem* to have. Our relationship canvas displays a picture of love, honor, and respect for each other. We often find ourselves saying "If you only knew how many messes we made along the way to this masterpiece on display."

We were approaching our 25th Anniversary in January of 2017. In December of 2016, I (Laura) shared 25 little-known facts on Facebook about our marriage journey, one a day at a time, until January 4th, 2017. I was surprised at the number of people who commented and said this was the highlight of their day. If I was late posting, I would get messages inquiring about the absent post. I finally decided to schedule the messages so I would not forget or get harassed by my followers for being slow. Our friends encouraged Wayne and me to write a book including some those "not-so-perfect" tales of our marriage journey.

It dawned on us that people wanted to see behind the curtains of this seemingly picture-perfect marriage. They wanted authenticity. We don't have the perfect marriage if such a thing even exists, but what we do have is built on love, trust, honor, and mutual respect and a sincere desire to reflect the image of God in our marriage.

To paint the most vivid and authentic picture of our marriage, we selected 51 moments in our 28-year-long relationship we felt impacted us the most. These are stories of our successes and failures, victories and defeat, joy, and pain. Each moment comes with a "shade", which are our lessons learned. We used the hashtag to acknowledge social media's role in the creation of the book. Each shade also encourages you to use various principles to create your own "shade" as you paint your marriage masterpiece. To get the most out this book, we encourage spouses to read the stories and complete the "shades" together. Grab a copy of 51 ½ Shades of Prayer to enhance your picture-perfect experience. The ½ shade is an acknowledgment that our masterpiece is still a work in progress.

Welcome to our life!

Beale AFB, California

1990-1994

1
Short-Sighted

April 1990

Laura – What would you think if the guy you've been eyeing all night ignores your invitation and pushes his friend toward you, instead? I was already struggling with a bit of low self-esteem at this point in my life and this night was not a confidence booster!

My first marriage had been a turbulent and bitter experience, filled with emotional and physical trauma. For years, I was told how inadequate I was in every way possible. My hair was never long enough, my teeth were never straight enough, my butt was not big enough. I heard, "If I don't want you, no other man would want you either." I walked on eggshells trying to avoid sparking any physical confrontation from the least of offenses. I am not ashamed to admit this had a hard-hitting effect on my self-worth; I started to believe what I heard day-in and day-out. I straddled the fence between disqualifying myself entirely, thinking I wasn't attractive, to overcompensating and trying to prove I was worth a second glance from the opposite sex.

This warm night on Beale AFB in California was one of those times I felt bold enough to put bait on the hook and see if any fish would bite. Well, not just any fish. It was one specific fish in the NCO Club "pond" I hoped to catch.

Wayne had friendly eyes, chocolate skin, a charming smile, and he was wearing bright red socks that caught my eyes whenever he walked toward the bar or leaned against the wall. This bright pop of color stood out in the otherwise dull atmosphere of the NCO Club. I had been giving him suggestive side-glances all night, to no avail! But I wasn't discouraged, yet—remember this was one of those nights I felt just bold enough to shoot my best shot. I finally saw my chance to talk to him, as I spotted him standing in the lobby of the club with his friend. The song "All Around the World" by Lisa Stansfield was pumping inside the dance area. I coyly stood next to Wayne, my head, and body bopping to the beat.

"I like this song," I said, casually. "I wish I had someone to dance with."

His response was not what I hoped. In fact, it was nothing like what I expected.

"Here, Ed, you dance with her!" he said, and forcefully shoved his friend toward me.

Both Ed and I were awkwardly speechless and surprised that Wayne would rather sacrifice his friend than give me a polite "No, thanks." With my ego in tatters, I rolled my eyes. I told myself the guy with the red socks was an idiot, and I strutted into the dance area without a partner.

Wayne – Uh-huh, okay. Here's how I remember the evening. My friend, Jerry, and I started out the night at Ed's house.

Ed was recently divorced, and we were trying to encourage him to go out, dance a little, have an enjoyable time, and maybe meet someone. He finally agreed to go to the NCO Club with us.

The place was jumping, but our only focus was to make sure Ed had a good time. I wasn't paying attention to any targets of engagement for myself. So, when a beautiful young lady walked by with a friend, I didn't give her a great deal of thought. I was there for Ed. Plus, she was too tall for me. I did the math in two seconds – I'm 5' 6" and she looked at least 5' 7" in flats. This meant she would be 5'10" in heels. Normally, I go for the 5'2" and under. What can I say? I thought I needed to see a woman looking up at me.

Fast forward past that two-second evaluation. The tall, beautiful woman says, "I really like this song."

I thought, "Cool, let's get Ed back in the game."

"Ed, she wants to dance," I told him, in my infinite wisdom. Now, you would be right in thinking I wasn't very good at taking hints. Just to give a little background, throughout my teens and young adult life, I continually missed subtle hints from young (and older) ladies. Perhaps it was God protecting me, saving me for the right moment... but probably not. I was just not the greatest at noticing those signals. I look back now and want to give myself the "Dunce of the Year" award for missing that moment in the club lobby. But it had more to do with how I saw myself versus how I saw Laura at that moment.

Laura – I judged his response by my own feelings of inadequacy because I had no clue of the mental hurdles he jumped over in two seconds. It seemed like he had rebuffed me, but instead, he had disqualified himself, thinking he wasn't enough to take me up on my offer. So, poor Ed became the scapegoat of the moment.

#OurShade – We both faced challenges in our confidence that night. Since then, we have learned to embrace and value our authentic selves, including whatever we bring to the table at the moment. We can never know what is going on in each other's head all the time (and we wouldn't want to know either.) We have learned not to assume what the other is thinking or to assume reasons for their actions (or lack of action).

#YourShade – On a separate sheet of paper, rate your spouse's confidence level on a scale of 1-10 in the areas listed on the chart on the following pages. Then, ask them to rate themselves. Record your answers on the chart by coloring in the squares with two different colors. See the example on the next page.

Compare the differences. What areas, if any, surprised you the most? Discuss what you can you do to help build your spouse's confidence where needed?

10								
9								
8								
7			■					
6			■					░
5			■	■				░
4			■	■			■	░
3	■		■	■			■	
2	■	■	■	■		■	■	■
1		■	■	■	■		■	■
	Physical Looks	Intellect	Personality	Spiritual Leader-ship	Sexual Skills	Parenting	Financial Provision	

In this example, the light color is how the wife **thinks** her husband feels about himself and the dark color is how the husband really feels about himself. What areas, if any, would you address with your spouse?

	Physical Looks	Intellect	Personality	Spiritual Leader-ship	Sexual Skills	Parenting	Other
10							
9							
8							
7							
6							
5							
4							
3							
2							
1							

	Physical Looks	Intellect	Personality	Spiritual Leader-ship	Sexual Skills	Parenting	Other
10							
9							
8							
7							
6							
5							
4							
3							
2							
1							

2
No Parking on the Dance Floor

Laura – Despite my "height handicap" we did end up dancing, but not because he braved up and asked me. Here's how it went down.

A few songs later, the DJ played "Doing Da Butt." I was on the floor dancing with a guy named Kevin, who was also the designated driver for the night. Mr. Red Socks was dancing with my friend Veronica, who came to the club with Kevin, another friend of ours named Julia, and me.

As the song was playing, before we realized what was happening, Kevin and Veronica started doing provocative dance moves – with each other! Kevin, Veronica, and I were friends, so I wasn't offended, but I was caught off guard. Wayne and I locked eyes, and in unspoken agreement, we decided we didn't want to get involved in the soft-porn dance show. So, we each started dancing away from them to give them their space, and he and I finally ended up dancing with each other.

When the song ended, a slow song came on – "Always and Forever," by Heatwave. We looked around and saw our previous dance partners exiting the floor together. Wayne and I stood on the dance floor, just looking at each other. Yeah, that was awkward.

"Do you slow dance?" I asked after the stillness started to get uncomfortable.

He quickly responded, "Well, since you asked me." What a cop out! It's a good thing I was feeling confident that night or his disinterest could have hurt my feelings!

Wayne – Hold up, wait a minute. Let me explain what was *really* going on here. I don't take "no" very well, so I didn't ask a young lady to slow dance unless I was pretty sure she'd say "yes."

I didn't quite know what was going on that night with Laura. By this time, we only had a brief time to talk. Actually, we hadn't talked at all. Laura had been dancing with a different guy, and I was also dancing with someone else. Next thing we knew, those two started dancing with each other. I didn't know they all knew each other! Laura and I looked at each other and decided, Why not? When the song ended, the DJ decided to slow things down. By that point, I absolutely knew I wanted to slow dance with Laura; however, I wasn't sure if the feeling was mutual. And yes, the height thing was still there. Once again, I found grace with Laura.

#OurShade – Personal internal conflicts caused us to make faulty assumptions about each other. This created faulty internal conversations in our minds before we had a chance to communicate with each other. Learn to silence your inner critic and engage in honest communication with your spouse.

#YourShade – What internal conversations do you have that stop you from communicating your desires to your spouse?

3
Who Let The Dogs Out?

Laura – Although our dance began awkwardly, we eventually found our rhythm, and we were able to relax and enjoy the moment. "Always and Forever" finished, and we sat to talk. The conversation was fun and easy. We were still talking when the "last call" rang through the club. I think Wayne was trying to redeem himself from rejecting me at first and then hedging on the dance request. Anyway, he suddenly came up with the brilliant pick up line.

"Um, excuse me, I just want to know if you take stray dogs home?" If your eyes are rolling now, imagine how I felt then! Sure, he deserved the award for the most idiotic pick-up line in the history of mankind. But I showed mercy and gave him my phone number and graciously accepted his. Why not, I thought.

But it wasn't smooth sailing yet. No, in fact, in gratitude for my kindness, Wayne made some bizarre hand gesture that knocked my purse out of my hand, sent it flying through the air, and spilled the entire contents of it across the floor of the club! Sorry, Wayne— no awards that night for being a smooth operator.

Wayne – Slow dancing was not my forte. I usually miss a step or two after two minutes. This time, I seemed to have found some sort of rhythm. I must admit, I did notice we did not see eye-to-eye while we danced. Despite that, my issue with Laura's height (or the lack of my height) continued to subside, and my confidence was boosted. We left the dance floor and sat down without needing to ask if we wanted to stick together or not. The conversation came easy. There was no need for me to try to be smooth. I don't remember what we talked about, only how much I enjoyed talking with this long-legged beauty.

By this time, I forgot about making sure Ed was doing okay. In fact, I forgot about most everything but her and me. The club was packed, but it seemed like our own space, and the rest of the club was just a backdrop for us. This was one of those times when you knew it would eventually end and the night would be over, but you wished it would continue.

Unfortunately, it had been a long day and a long night, and, I had reached my quota of words. It was a stimulating, honest conversation, and by the end of the night, giving any kind of "line" was probably the worst I could say to such a remarkable woman. I did it anyway because I didn't know what else to say. In addition to delivering a "playa from the Himalaya" line, when I reached out to Laura for a goodbye hug or handshake, my aim was way off, and I smacked her purse clean out of her hand. This seemed like two strikes, at least. I thought all was lost and tried my best to help her pick up the contents of her purse. I cautiously handed her the items from the floor. Somehow it seemed too intimate to be handling her personal items. Some ladies can be protective about such things. I kept thinking to myself, over and over "Real smooth, Wayne, real smooth."

#OurShade – Sometimes our best intentions can go sideways. It took us time to learn how to keep our composure and most importantly, learn to laugh at ourselves! We learned if we laugh first, it may keep others laughing with us versus laughing at us.

#YourShade – When was the last time your or your spouse's good intentions didn't go as planned? How did you respond? Did you assume the best or the worst? What would you do differently?

4
Things You Learn in the Backseat

"Oh! What a tangled web we weave when first we practice to deceive" - Sir Walter Scott

Laura – The club closed, and I got into the car of the designated driver for the night, Kevin. Veronica and I hopped into the back seat, and our other friend Julia sat in the front seat.

Without a word of warning, Wayne brazenly jumped into the back seat of the car, next to me. All of us ladies were surprised, but Kevin wasn't.

Wayne must have sensed my shock and discomfort from him jumping in the backseat with me. Maybe it was my sideways glance or the way my eyes widened in disbelief that gave me away.

He patted Kevin on the shoulder and said, "It's okay, Kevin and I know each other." I could tell he wanted to reassure me that he wasn't a crazy person. "Tell her how we know each other, man," he urged Kevin.

It turned out Kevin had a close connection to Wayne. Kevin quietly offered up an explanation,

"Pam is Wayne's ex-wife."

Kevin and Pam were living together up until two weeks before this night.

Coincidentally, I was connected to Pam, through Kevin. I was a Dental Technician in the Air Force, and Pam was headed to the Air Force, and after basic training, she would go to school for Dental Technician training. Kevin asked me if she could borrow my training books to get a feel for what to expect. I gladly loaned her my books—after all, I wasn't using them anymore!

I also had a chance to meet her before she left, because Kevin asked me to babysit his son so Pam and he could enjoy some alone time before she left. When I went over to his house to pick up his son, Pam answered the door. We quickly exchanged pleasantries, and I left with Kevin's son. I didn't think I'd ever see or hear about her again.

What a tangled web, don't you think? But wait, there are even more layers to the web!

The plot thickened, as we also discovered Wayne had an unexpected connection with me. We were all talking in the car, cheerful and excited from a night of dancing, and Veronica mentioned that people think her son and Wayne's son look alike. I discovered Wayne and Veronica knew each other because she knew his ex-wife, Pam.

Wayne showed me a picture of his six-year-old son, Aurelius (aka Real) and his eight-year-old daughter, Ouidaintria (aka Ouidii), and I made a mental note to give him two points for having a picture of his children in his wallet. I agreed his son resembled Veronica's son, and then I showed him a picture of my five-year-old daughter, LaTasha (aka Tasha). This is where things got sticky.

Wayne glanced at my daughter's picture, then he gave a puzzled look and stared at it more carefully.

"Wait, I know this little girl," he exclaimed.

I became equally as puzzled as he looked.

"Really, how?" I asked.

"She comes to track practice with my children's track coach. He is always talking about her mom, and how much he loves her, and they are getting married soon." After a brief, but revelatory pause, Wayne asked, "Is that you?"

I felt as if every eye in the car was on me. Probably because every eye in the car was on me. I felt them all waiting for me to say something, so I gave the only response I could.

"Yep, that would be me."

Wayne gave a sly grin and said, "Alrighty then…y'all have a good night."

Wayne patted Kevin on his shoulder again and hopped out of the car and dashed across the parking lot to his car. My friends didn't even wait for him to close the door before they began howling with laughter at me.

#OurShade – Thank goodness, since then, neither of us had to navigate our way through past entanglements. Oh, believe us, we know how uncomfortable or embarrassing it can be. But we had to expose these things quickly and honestly, or there was a real chance they could have hindered us from moving forward with a healthy relationship. I think of it as ripping off the Band-Aid!

#YourShade – Find a knotted jewelry chain or get a piece of rope, ribbon, or fishing twine and make several knots and loops to tangle it. Set a timer for two minutes. Working together with your eyes closed, try to untangle the chain (or ribbon/rope/twine). Now try it again with your eyes open. Discuss the difference (if any), in the results.

What past entanglements do you need to address, with eyes wide open, as a couple (relationships, debts, habits, fears...)?

5
Three's Company – Six is Wild

Laura – Wayne and I were both full-time, single parents when we met— the black version of the Brady Bunch! His two plus my one made three, so, our first "date" included our kids and us, which made five, and one surprise guest.

Wayne – Laura called me a couple of days after we met. I was shocked she still wanted to talk to me after my shabby attempt at being smooth. I was interested in her and would have called her first, except I didn't write her name on the paper with her phone number. I didn't want to embarrass myself further by not remembering her name! At this point, before she called, I figured my chances of getting to know Laura better were dwindling fast. Yet by the grace of God, she decided to give me yet another chance, even after I told her the reason I didn't call first was because I forgot her name.

It was always easy for us to talk to each other, and after several phone conversations, we finally planned a date.

Now, I'm not one to introduce my kids to everyone I meet. However, Laura was someone I definitely wanted them to meet. She was someone I wanted to get to know better.

The day of the date came. I told the kids we were going

to eat pizza at a friend's house. Fortunately, "pizza for dinner" was all they needed to hear. They were excited about the menu and didn't care about the venue. The date was informal, so we didn't have to change into "nice" clothes. We all got in the car, drove to pick up pizza, and headed over to Laura's house. Keep in mind I didn't have much experience letting anyone get that close to my kids. Therefore, I had no clue how the evening would go. When we arrived at the house, Laura came to the door with this funny look. I'm thinking, "Dang, here we go! She's about to treat me like a dirty shoe and give me the brush off". Instead, Laura told me we may have a "situation," specifically, that Adonis, Laura's fiancé was there.

I'm now thinking she's going to ask me to leave and not cause a scene, or, ask me to come back later. Imagine my surprise when she did neither and asked me if I still wanted to come in. For some strange reason, I decided to go by the vampire's code. You know how that goes? I can enter only if invited. Therefore, since she invited me into her home, I needed to stay. Plus, I had the kids with me so I couldn't disappoint them.

So, there we were–all six of us sitting in Laura's living room. The kids were oblivious to the uncomfortable situation of the adults around them. For the adults, the word "uncomfortable" does not even began to describe the next couple of hours.

The three kids hit it off right away. They were already

familiar with one another from track practice. For them, the adults were just the people providing the food and entertainment. They were more focused on watching the movie. The adults were… well, we were trying to act like adults. We made small talk and tried to pretend this awkward situation was normal. I can truly say it felt unique, weird, and downright scandalous. It also makes for a lively chapter in this book.

Laura – Did he say awkward? That doesn't begin to describe what I felt when Wayne agreed to come in, with his two little ones.

You're probably wondering, how does a girl entertain her fiancé, three kids (two of them complete strangers), and a potential love interest? She doesn't! The night took care of itself. Even though my house had enough room for everyone to spread out, I felt like one of those toys in a claw-grabber machine. The kids were on the floor, engrossed in their movie. Wayne and my fiancé, who already knew each other, had an unspoken beer-drinking competition which eventually led to them both falling asleep in separate chairs. Wayne sat on the couch in the center of the living room, and Adonis, perhaps recognizing his fading position in my life, sat in the back corner of the living room in an oversized Papasan chair.

In the meantime, Veronica and one of my other girlfriends had both called, at separate times, to ask if I would babysit while they went to the club with their husbands. I had no other plans than being at home (with "Bob & Nod" on the couch), so I figured, why not? The more, the merrier, as they say! My friends arrived at different times. It was funny how each of them sized up the room. First, they looked at the men asleep in their chairs, and then they each gave me a puzzled look.

"Can I speak to you in private?" both asked. Their main question was the exact same thing…

"Laura, what the hell are you doing?"

My response was also the same.

"The hell if I know!

All they could do was shake their heads and give me an "I hope you know what you are doing" look. They wished me luck and left to enjoy their evening at the club.

After the men woke up from their beer-battle induced nap, it was clear neither of them would offer to leave on his own. I told Wayne it would be best if he left first, and then wait for my call to return, and he obliged. After the first movie was over, he gathered his children and said his good-byes to Adonis, the other children, and me. To my surprise, Adonis had little to say after Wayne left. I was prepared with my shameless defense of, "oh, we are only friends, letting the kids hang out together." Adonis asked no questions, even though I sensed he had quite a few. We had some small talk, and he left. After Adonis left, I called Wayne to give him his "come back cue," and he and the kids returned to finish the movie date.

I know our story is off to a shady start. You could say it paints a vivid picture of distrust, disrespect, and underhandedness. You would not be wrong to feel "some type of way" about Wayne and me at this point. You might even want to give us a side glance. I would too.

The story doesn't end here, and I like to think we all did what we could to make the best of a tricky situation. Obviously, I broke off the engagement, and yes, I returned the ring, too. And even though it was the right thing for Wayne and me to be together, it doesn't mean we never felt remorseful about how things happened. Adonis was a nice guy, and neither of us has one negative word to say about him. It just wasn't meant for us to be together. I have never regretted choosing Wayne; I only regret the way I handled the situation with Adonis.

In 2008, 18 years after that bizarre date night, I saw Adonis on the social media website MySpace. I wanted to reach out to him and apologize. I talked with Wayne before I reached out to Adonis, and he agreed. I wrote a letter of apology to him. I didn't apologize for the breakup, I apologized for the way it happened. I took total responsibility for what happened and asked him to forgive me for any hurt it caused him. He also apologized for whatever he may have done to hurt me (which was nothing, really). This simple action removed the weight of guilt I carried for years.

As divine timing would have it, Wayne deployed to Iraq in 2008, and he was in the same area as Adonis. Wayne reached out and called him. I don't know the specifics of the conversation, and I didn't feel like it was my right to know. We each had our own relationship with Adonis before we met. We both had to come to terms with our roles and actions in the breakup and our responsibility to reconcile that relationship.

Adonis and I remain connected through Facebook. I am pleased to report he is now happily married to a beautiful woman and has a lovely family.

#OurShade – Listening to your Ego will lead you to places where confidence would tell you to leave. I (Laura) had a lack of confidence Wayne would return if I told him to leave when he first arrived at the door, which led to that strange afternoon. Wayne let his ego lead him into a tangled web competing with Adonis when he could have left with confidence that I would want to see him again.

#YourShade – Recount the times in your marriage when you allowed your ego to make the decision (arguments, financial decisions, etc.) versus leading with confidence and wisdom. How would those decisions have looked with confidence leading the way?

What major decisions are you facing now? What is your plan to silence your ego in the decision-making process?

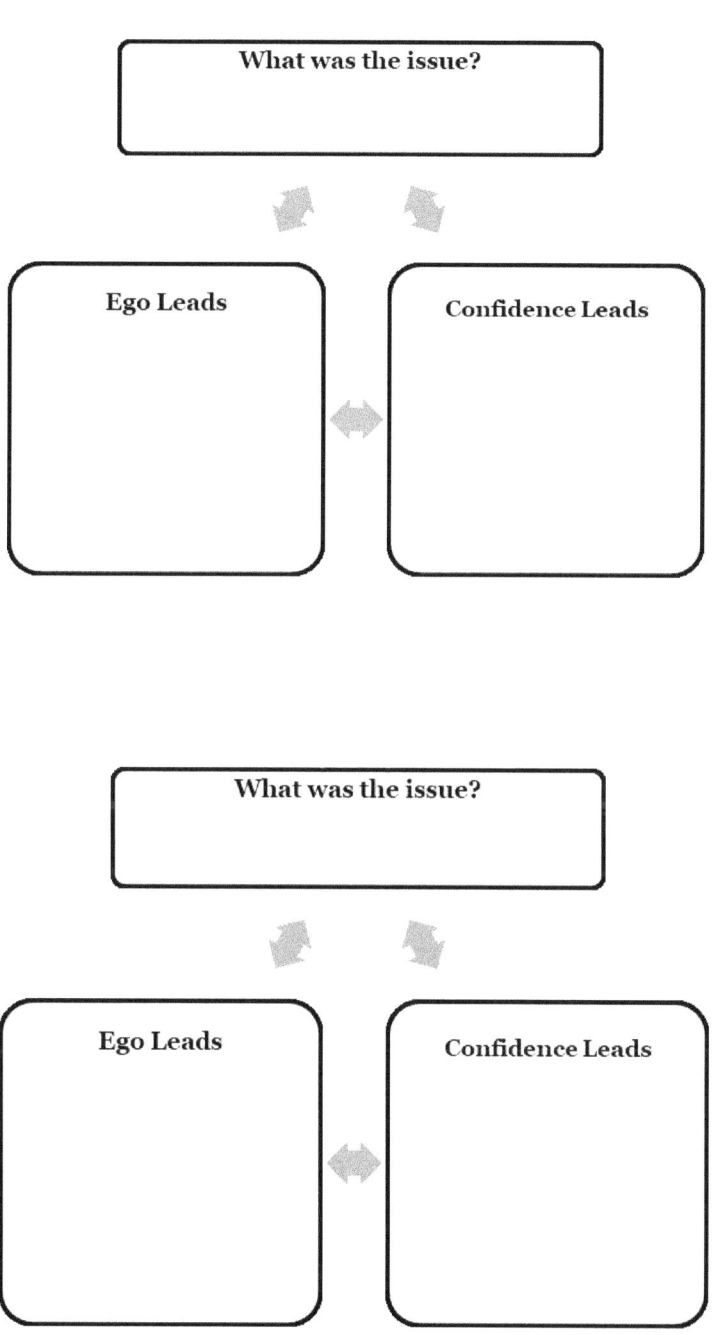

6
Hidden in Plain Sight

Laura – There was a rumor the hospital on Beale, Air Force Base in California had some of the prettiest women on base. Everyone knew about the "three black chicks" in the dental clinic. That would be Stephanie, Valerie, and me. Whenever we went to the club, whether together or separately, and someone asked where we worked (which is a common question most military members ask each other), and we'd say, "the Dental Clinic," the response was "Oh, y'all the ones!"

The Dental Clinic wasn't a large place and consisted of one long corridor with several dental treatment rooms and a lobby. Each dental tech had to walk down the corridor and enter the lobby to get our patients. We had a chance to see nearly every patient scheduled throughout the day.

Wayne already knew Stephanie and Valerie. Although Wayne visited the Dental Clinic twice a year, our paths never crossed. I think God was hiding me until he was ready for such a gift... that's my story, and I'm sticking to it.

Wayne – There was indeed a rumor. All a young man had to do was go check. The hospital had several areas with attractive ladies. Many of us would stop at the hospital for the smallest ailment. As soon as we felt a scratchy throat or watery eyes, we would head to the hospital in hopes of receiving some needed medication, or something to ease the pain.

The dental clinic, which was in the hospital, was like icing on the cake. Most people on base went to the dental clinic at least twice a year. Some had to go more often because of their lack of dental hygiene. Since I was too afraid to make up a fake toothache, I was one of the twice-a-year people. With my luck, I would end up with a root canal.

Now that I think about it, more examples of "in plain sight" are the facts that...

...Laura and I lived within five minutes of each other,

...our children went to the same schools,

...we were at the club at the same time on many occasions. It was the only club on the base, so most people were there every weekend.

#OurShade – Sometimes the best things in life are hidden in plain sight, and we can miss them if we aren't paying attention! We can lose focus in marriage and miss the beauty of the treasures hidden in plain sight. Even worse, we can get so entangled in the daily business of work, parenting, ministry, and other activities that we lose the desire to even search for the treasure in our spouses and our marriage. We try to take time to focus on the hidden treasures in each other and in our partnership

#YourShade – Draw a treasure chest and fill it with the

words or images that describe the treasures in your marriage and/or in your spouse. Take time to tell your spouse how much you appreciate and value the gifts they bring to your marriage.

7
The Writing on the Wall

Wayne – As I talked about earlier, the first visit to Laura's house was quite interesting. The next visit was just as interesting. As soon as we walked in, I noticed a metal sign hanging on the wall in the entranceway. Somehow, I missed this on my first visit. In summary, the sign read:

Kiss Me, F___k Me, Tell Me You Love Me, then Get the Hell Out!

When I first saw it, I thought it was humorous. I chuckled. Then I asked myself, "Why would she have this type of sign"? Her daughter, Tasha, was five years old and was just learning to read, so the sign didn't register in her five-year-old mind. However, my daughter, Ouidii was eight years old, curious, and she could read very well. As we passed the sign, Ouidii began to read it out loud. I looked at Laura, and she looked at me. What do you do? This was B.C. (before Christ), so I didn't think to ask, "What would Jesus do"?

But imagine what I must have been thinking to myself when I walked into the hallway and read the sign (I'm glad I could read, too). The mischievous side of me displayed a devilish grin. Another side, maybe the wiser-side, was more cautious and wondered, "what I done got myself into?" In the middle was a boyish curiosity. With 2-out-of-3 odds, it was a win-win for me. Everyone laughed, and Laura took the sign down without making a big scene.

Laura – I was going through a defiantly free stage in my life. I was tired of being the "good girl." I started dressing to reflect this new-found free me. (I even had a "man-catcher" skirt which worked perfectly.) I was a frequent shopper at Spencer's, an adult-themed gift shop where you could buy all sorts of scandalous and sexually explicit items. I once bought a lapel pin that spelled "BITCH," and wore it with pride

I thought it was cool and rebellious, after spending five days a week in a military uniform of bright white nurse's gear, nude stockings, and cushioned loafers. My friends thought it was cool too, so how it could it be wrong? I gave no thought to my daughter because she was too young to read the sign with full understanding or contemplate her mommy's actions.

The day Wayne's daughter read that sign was a wake-up call for me. The whole "free me" attitude instantly became one of regret and embarrassment! I removed the sign and threw it into the trash that day. Wayne forgot to mention the handcuffs that went along with the sign. Don't ask about the handcuffs. I am grateful it did not scare Wayne away from pursuing the relationship, but maybe I should have questioned why he wasn't scared.

#OurShade – Sometimes we do or say things, and we think it's cute, funny, or cool. As time goes on, it's not as cute, funny, or cool to our spouses anymore. This wasn't an issue for Laura only—there are things Wayne let go for Laura, too! Although that sign was funny then.

Our Example – During premarital counseling, we had to list some annoying habits of our partner. Wayne confessed that my habit of not putting the cassette tapes back in their cases annoyed him. It seemed trivial to me, but it was important to him. If I had not discovered this, it could have been a point of contention in our marriage.

#YourShade – What does your spouse do that you tolerated, but now you wish they stop doing it? We encourage you to discuss it with your spouse and reach an agreement about needed adjustments.

8
Check Your Bags at the Door

Wayne – Laura and I met in April, and two months later I took my kids to their grandparents for the summer. I had been out of town for a few weeks and was glad to get back home after a dreary 2,600-mile drive. When I got home, I unpacked and took a breather. When I got up, I decided to relax at a friend's house. A couple of other friends came over, and we were chillin'.

Suddenly, one of my friends craned his head to look out a window, and he asked, "Isn't that Laura's car cruising by?" I didn't see the car, so I couldn't answer. Something felt strange, so after a few minutes, I called Laura. Her short answers and flat tone were clues that she was angry about something, but even with those clues, I was clueless.

"Is something wrong?"

"How long have you been home?"

"Uhm, a few hours, I guess."

"Why didn't you call me when you got home?"

"I didn't realize I needed to call."

Wrong answer, Wayne, wrong answer!

I didn't understand this was about something more than relationship protocol. There was a trust issue underlying the situation. Perhaps Laura had to deal with someone lying and cheating. I didn't know, but I should have thought about it. Instead, I was justifying not needing to call her first. If I called when I got home, it would let her know she was higher on the list of people to see than my friends. I am happy to say this mistake has not happened again in over 26 years.

Laura – Yes, I was dealing with trust and rejection issues from past relationships. I had not dealt with my old baggage, and it traveled with me from relationship to relationship.

In my defense, most of my past relationships only served to add to my baggage of distrust. Wayne and I hadn't been dating long enough for him to recognize my baggage, help me unpack those bags and, more importantly, toss them in the trash.

#OurShade – We each have a past. Until we have passed the past, we are stuck with little hope for a future. We learned through this that it's not enough to only be mindful of our own baggage. We also need to recognize each other's baggage, and we must be willing to help each other unpack it also. It's also vital we don't start adding more weight to the baggage either. Over our years together, we've learned to recognize the signs of "unchecked baggage," and we handle it at once. We also avoid blaming each other for the baggage we brought to the relationship.

What are some signs of "unchecked baggage"?

- Unwarranted fears of abandonment

- Projection of insecurities
- Constant accusations
- Snooping (phone, email, pockets, etc.)
- Negative comparison to past relationships (silently or verbally)
- Unreasonable expectations
- Unresolved anger

#YourShade – What baggage from your past relationships (romantic, family, friendships, etc.) are you holding onto today?
- What baggage do see your spouse holding on to?
- What effect does it have on your current relationship?
- How can you help each other unpack your baggage?

9
Exes and Ohs!

Wayne – Jerome, a "friend" of Laura's, was one of those charismatic, Billy Dee-type fellas. Because Laura had already told me about the nature of their "friendship," I automatically saw him as a competitor. Therefore, he was not my friend, and I wasn't trying to be his. After meeting him, I realized we could have hung out together. He and I never had any beef between us. However, the fact that Laura mentioned him a bit too much for my taste meant he was the enemy. At least that's how I thought about it.

Jerome became a suitable scapegoat for me hide my insecurities about myself and our relationship. For example, instead of saying how I felt about myself, I could focus on Jerome and tell Laura she had feelings she needed to address. How crazy is that?! Not crazy at all. A little immature or irrational, but not crazy.

As Laura and I discussed it, I realized my beef was with Wayne, and I needed to take care of it quickly. I thank God for giving me someone who is willing to accept me and help me work through my flaws.

Laura -Wayne was not the only one with self-acceptance issues. I recall a day a few months into our relationship when I was over at his house, enjoy my time with him. That screeched to a halt when Pam, his ex-wife, stopped by upon her return from military basic training and asked him to check out some issue she was having with her vehicle. I felt threatened by her presence and especially by his willingness to help her with her car issue.

It never occurred to me to be grateful for a gracious and thoughtful man, who despite their differences, was adult enough to help his ex-wife in this situation. When he went outside to help her, my mind was racing with a plethora of questions like "Why is she asking him? What are her motives? Where is Kevin? Why is Wayne helping her…?"

Of course, I was wise enough not to just go out there and stand guard like the insecure and jealous girlfriend I was. What I did do was to stand on top of the toilet and station myself near the bathroom window which faced the driveway. From my porcelain post, I was able to covertly hear and see if anything went sideways. To my surprise, my five-year-old daughter, Tasha, was bolder than I was. She went outside and stood to watch until his ex-wife left.

#OurShade – Our insecurities and low self-esteem caused us to project our worries and fears upon each other, and this got us into some awkward positions (Like Laura standing on the toilet!). We do our best to expose those areas, own them, and expel them swiftly. We now understand the true source of our worth can only come from the One who created us in His image.

#YourShade – What internal fears or self-acceptance issues do you have that you deflect upon your spouse? What one thing (or more) can your spouse do to dispel your worries?

10
Shut The Front Door

Wayne – The summer of '89 was pretty good. I was recently divorced and headed to my 10-year class reunion. A newly single brother who was taking care of two young children, and had a steady job with benefits, was a pretty good catch. And I knew it. I was okay with the attention from the opposite sex. After that summer, my self-esteem was high. My kids and I were in sync; we had developed a solid routine, but it didn't leave much room for anyone else.

Fast forward nine months, and by chance, I meet Laura, this beautiful woman with whom I loved to spend time in her company. We shared the same interests, we were dedicated single parents, and we both were employed by the US Air Force…seems like a pretty good match to me.

However, I wasn't sure if I really wanted to be exclusive versus inclusive. The upcoming summer trip to Georgia would answer that question.

Before I left California, I stopped by Laura's house to let her know I was leaving. Truth be told, I felt a pull to stay in California. This pull was coming from feelings within me, not from any pressure by Laura. As I drove home to Georgia (which took three days), I spent most of the time thinking about Laura and our time together. I was thinking about her so much that when I got home, my Momma and sister noticed I was behaving differently than the previous time I came home, for my class reunion.

While I was home, I visited one of my classmates who I had reconnected with the previous summer. We went to dinner and a movie, which is a date night by most standards. Since I wasn't one to lie about relationships, as we talked, I told her about Laura. The rest of the night went well, or so I thought. I must have acted disinterested or distracted, because the next day when I went to revisit her, she asked me a direct question, "Do you love her?" I didn't know how serious my feelings were for Laura. I tried to play as if the question didn't hit me like a blow from Mike Tyson. But my stuttering and inability to find words made it clear Laura was not a casual acquaintance.

Later that day my sister looked at me and said it was time for me to cut my visit short and head back to California. It was apparent to her I wanted to be with Laura more than I wanted to visit with family. As I look back, when my classmate asked the defining question, the door was closed; then my sister was the one to make sure I didn't try to reopen it.

Laura – Like Wayne said, he was never one to lie about relationships. He was honest enough to share with me the information about a relationship he was considering with an ex-classmate in his hometown. I knew he was going home on leave only a couple of months after we met. He told me he would let "the other woman" know about his relationship with me.

With everything within me, I tried to keep the ever-present green-eyed monster under tight surveillance. I remember trying to be the "bigger person" and giving him his freedom while home on leave to sort things out. At least that's what my mouth said, but my heart was not in agreement. He was going on vacation for three weeks. My mind went into overdrive imagining all the scenarios that could take place in twenty-one days and hundreds of miles away from my sight. I had to trust, blindly trust, he would make the right decisions.

Because some things are best left unknown, I never asked what happened. I knew I wasn't emotionally mature or secure enough to hear any details. Plus, I wanted to keep my word about giving him "freedom" to handle it. In fact, I am learning along with you, the reader, what happened. What I do know is, twenty-eight years later we are still here to tell our story.

More Doors

Laura – When your past, present, and potential future relationships exist in the same zip code, life becomes one critical decision after another. I know you are thinking, "But Laura, you broke it off with your ex-fiancé, didn't you?" Yes, I did, and it was a clean break. Yet there was one more door left ajar in my past.

Closing doors was not my method of operation. Most of my relationships ended like a month-old carton of milk–never finished, just simply expired, sitting doing nothing in the back of the fridge. My usual modus operandi was to transition from one relationship to another (I forgot to mention, even though I was engaged to Adonis, I was still married to my first husband, but that's another long story for another time).

And then there was my friend Jerome…I met Jerome about a year before I met Wayne. Actually, I met Jerome before I met Adonis (but that's also another story for a different time). While the two of us never officially dated, we did have an intimate relationship over the course of those two years. There was a mutual understanding of "my door was always open." No strings, no pressure, no expectations.

When I met Wayne, unbeknownst to Jerome, all that changed. Jerome was soon deployed to Kuwait during the Gulf War, so that half-open door was almost forgotten. But then Wayne had to go away for school for several weeks for training at March AFB in Riverside, CA, and as timing would have it, Wayne's trip happened just as Jerome returned from his deployment in the desert. He called to let me know he was back in town. He didn't know about Wayne and probably hoped he'd be returning to our "open door" policy.

The day of reckoning had come. I had to trust myself to

make the right decision, and I had to have the conviction that a relationship with Wayne is what I truly wanted. Out of courtesy and respect for Wayne, I did inform him I was going to meet with Jerome to settle the situation and officially close that door. I am sure Wayne's mind was going down several rabbit holes, especially since he was hundreds of miles away in southern California.

He had nothing to worry about! (Easy for to me say, right?) When I met with Jerome, I shared my heart about my relationship with Wayne, and he understood how Wayne was different than the others I had dated (he saw a couple come and go). He commented he wondered who had stolen my attention so much so, that I didn't write him while he was deployed. Without any pressure, he bowed out gracefully and has never tried to "jiggle the lock" to see if the door was indeed closed.

I can say with absolute surety, I have never regretted, even for a moment, my decision to close the door on my past and move forward with Wayne. Neither of us knew what the future held for us regarding our relationship, but I knew if I wanted to look toward a future, the door to the past had to be closed with a resounding thud! Jerome and I are casually connected on Facebook and occasionally will comment on each other's posts. I even took the time to give him a heads up about his inclusion in our stories. True to his character, he found it an honor to be significant enough to make the cut in one of our stories.

#OurShade – Our future remained obscured until we were willing to close the doors of our past relationships. We made the decision to move forward and didn't look back.

#YourShade – What doors to your past need closing? How will you close them?

11
Rain Dance Romance

Nothing says romance like pushing a car in the rain.

Laura – Wayne had to go away to the NCO Academy for leadership training at March AFB in Riverside, CA. I took the opportunity to visit him by catching a ride with a couple of friends who were heading that way. The discomfort of riding 500 miles in the backseat of a pickup truck was a small price to pay to see him for a weekend.

Wayne planned a romantic evening for my arrival. He borrowed a friend's car and met me at a designated meeting spot. With excitement in the air and romance on our minds, we didn't want to waste any time getting our evening of romance started.

Unfortunately, the borrowed car had other plans and broke down shortly after we headed to our room! Wayne tried to restart it a few times, all unsuccessful. We couldn't just leave it by the side of the road, so we decided to push the car to a safe spot in an empty parking lot. It started raining, which, mixed with the chill in the air, made it a miserable start to what was supposed to be a romantic reunion.

Out of breath from pushing a broke down car, cold, wet, and laden with luggage, we tried to focus on a warm, leisurely night together in the room Wayne reserved on base.

We walked about a mile to the lodging area, encouraged by those thoughts of a warm room and a place to set down my luggage. We reached the door and felt a wave of comfort, but only for a moment. Wayne opened the door to discover it already occupied (oops). There had been a misunderstanding with the reservation, and this room was double-booked.

Still wet, still cold, still burdened with luggage, we walked to the registration building. It was quite some distance away from the lodging area–it felt like several miles. After they assigned us another room, we made the hike back to the lodging area and found the new room. By this time, it was dark, even colder, and still raining. We were tired, cold, wet, and hungry. All we could get to eat at that hour was a tasteless, cardboard-like pizza and a two-liter bottle of soda. Somehow, we still managed to laugh about the whole situation.

Wayne – As I look back, why in the Sam Hill did I borrow that Model T? Well, my friend wanted to help and save me the money for a rental or paying for a taxi. He wasn't using his car that weekend and wanted to help a brother out. However, because I didn't have a backup or another friend to call, we were "stuck like Chuck." The fiasco at the lodging area wasn't my fault, but it was my responsibility to find a room. I almost broke out in dance when we found out there were other rooms available. I don't even want to think about what it might have been like if everything was booked! Anyway, between the car and the lodging, you best believe after that night, I had a backup to the backup.

#OurShade – When things didn't go as planned, we made the best of those moments anyway! It is easy to find joy when we are looking for it.

#YourShade – What things in your marriage are not going as planned? Take a moment and discover the joy hidden inside of those moments.

12
The Run Around

Laura - Our relationship is battle-tested. It almost ended because of a 1 ½ mile run around a track.

A few weeks before this debacle, I failed my Air Force fitness test which included a 1 ½ mile run in under fifteen minutes. After failing it once, I had sixty days to get my act together and retake the test.

I shared my frustration with Wayne, and he volunteered to help me train and conquer the run. We decided to use the track around the football field on base as my practice field. It was a quarter mile around, so I needed to run around it seven times. Wayne ran next to me, helping me set the pace. All went well until the third lap when I became nauseous and short of breath. The pain in my legs and the burning feeling in my chest were obvious signs, to me, we should stop for a minute.

I admit I was out of shape! Between heaving pants, I told him I couldn't breathe. In his best drill-sergeant voice he responded,

"If you can talk, you can breathe!"

Not to be undone, I clutched my chest and described a burning pain, trying to convince him I was unwell.

"I know CPR," he responded slyly. "I'll get a medal for

saving you, too. Keep it moving." I began to rethink my relationship with such a cruel and heartless taskmaster. I was fueled by anger and unbelief as I finished my laps for the day. But I had to put the anger behind me a few more times because I still needed Wayne's help to pass my run test.

Wayne – The start of a relationship is a tricky time. You must maneuver through feelings and emotional landmines. I guess I stepped on an IED (improvised explosive device) that time. Experience should have told me to tread lightly. Instead, I rushed ahead to "help" Laura make her time.

In my mind, I was going to save the day and become the hero. So, like any hero, I pressed forward and started barking out orders, I mean, "encouragement." I thought Laura's face was flushed red from the heat of running. WRONG! She was red with fury, especially when she had to listen to Sergeant Brown's rendition of "Move Something."

By the time I realized how far I had gone into the minefield, it was too late. The only thing I could do was blow myself up and hope she didn't do what she probably was thinking.

Laura – We survived that moment, and the upside of it was I made my run time a few weeks later. I even had enough time to spare to jog back onto the dreaded track to encourage a friend who was struggling with her time.

#OurShade – There have been times when we failed to encourage each other in the way we wanted or needed to be encouraged. Sometimes we tried to justify it as tough love, but, it was just insensitive and ineffective. Now, we try to encourage each other in a way that makes us better and drives us closer to our goals. It helps that our many years together have made us fluent in each other's "love language." Knowing your partner's love language, personality, temperament, and their *lead language go a long way in figuring out what type of encouragement we need.

#YourShade – What is your love language? Is it words of affirmation, quality time, receiving gifts, acts of service, or physical touch? (For more information on love languages go to www.5lovelanguages.com)

How can you use love languages to encourage and motivate each other to reach your goals?

Challenge – Write a note of encouragement to your spouse each day this week.

To find out more about Lead Languages, ask about our Dream Team Workshop!

13
Waterbed Rumble

What could be more fun than an unexpected rollercoaster ride in the middle of the night?

Laura – Wayne and I were asleep. It was the middle of the night and darkness enveloped the room. We had a waterbed (yeah, a long time ago). The warmth of the bed and gentle swaying motion made for a peaceful sleep. Peaceful, that is, until the night my six-year-old daughter, Tasha, decided to enter our room with ninja-like stealth and patience. She had a bad dream and was seeking comfort. She came into the room and silently stood over me.

Even though I didn't hear her, I must have felt her presence because I suddenly opened my eyes. In the dark, my mind was suspended somewhere between the haze of sleep and a surprised, what in the hell! I could only make out a looming shadow standing over me. Come on now, what do you think I did? Precisely what any rational person would do – I screamed. No, I mean I really screamed! My scream startled Tasha and she joined the screaming.

The screams aroused Wayne from his sleep. What did he do? What any rational man would do! It was dark, and he was unable to see what threat of danger engulfed us, so he joined the scream fest and screamed too—a man-scream of course— and reached out to pull me away from this unseen danger. Tasha was holding on to me, so she came along for the ride as Wayne snatched us, still screaming, to safety. But safety is a wobbly illusion when everyone is screaming and bouncing up and down on a waterbed mattress!

Once we all regained our composure and the bed stopped moving like a tidal wave, we were all panting from the excitement. Wayne turned on the lamp next to the bed and just stared at us, not saying a word. I guess he was part-baffled and part-upset we activated "The Protector" for no reason. It didn't help that my daughter and I couldn't stop laughing at the absurdity of it all. I am sure our neighbors, who were only a thin wall away, contemplated calling the police!

Wayne – "Aroused" is a good word, but not good enough. Webster defines aroused as "to stir to action or strong response." There was no stirring. It was more like "shocking." At that moment, the words from the "Friday the 13th" movie were in my head, "kill-kill, kill-kill." Imagine waking up from a deep sleep, full of adrenaline pumping, and then finding out there was no threat. Well, what would you do?

#OurShade – Sometimes life brings us unexpected encounters, and we experience a temporary loss of stability. We always remember to safeguard what's most important (each other!), even if we don't fully understand the situation.

#YourShade – What area(s) in your marriage seems unstable right now (finances, health, intimacy, etc.)? What immediate steps can you take to protect your marriage and each other while working on those areas?

14
Proposal Gone Wrong

Laura – As Bart Simpson is my witness, this is a true story. After a year of dating, Wayne asked me to marry him while we were watching the Simpsons, with NO ring!

Wayne – Let me address the "NO RING" part. Truthfully, there is no excuse. I knew I wanted to marry Laura, but I was still a little gun shy. It was like that first slow dance together, all over again! Also, I had already jacked up one marriage and didn't want to go two-for-two.

Even though I thought and hoped my first marriage would last; my thoughts were not enough to make it last. It survived much longer on paper than it did in reality. With that in mind, my weak attempt landed me in the "Simpleton's Hall of Fame." It's mind-boggling how in my profession and career, I was bold and led many people. Then in another area of life, which is, unfortunately, my love life, I suffered from arrested development.

This is a roundabout way of explaining to you that I didn't have a ring because I kept going back and forth on "ask" and "don't ask." By the time I finally made up my mind, I didn't want to wait for the RIGHT time.

Laura – My first response was the "stank" face. Why? Because while we were watching the Simpsons, he was talking about buying the van he wanted, then suddenly and unbeknownst to me, he shifted the topic. He said he wanted me to be a Brown—THAT was the whole proposal! But the way he slipped it in with no fanfare, I totally missed the topic shift in our conversation. I thought I heard him say he wanted the van to be brown and I just didn't like the thought of an ugly brown van!

Once I figured out what he was asking, I said yes. My joy was all the greater after switching from the idea of an ugly brown van to the prospect of a life together forever. My joy only lasted a few seconds because Wayne's seven-year-old son, Real, came into the living room, crying and holding his stomach. Why? His older sister, Ouidii, punched him…because he called her a bitch…and so begins the next phase in our adventure!

Wayne – As far as my kids go, those two liked and disliked each other several times a day. Perhaps I should have let them know about the proposal ahead of time and made sure they would be on their best behavior. I guess this interruption was a sign of things to come.

To be honest, I wasn't quite sure if Laura loved me, felt sorry for me, or a little bit of both. Either way, I'm glad she said yes and decided to come down the aisle January 4, 1992. I'd certainly preferred to be married to Laura than to a brown van.

#OurShade – We could spend time waiting for the perfect

time and end up missing the opportune time to make a life-changing decision. Instead, we always embrace the moment and move forward.

#YourShade – What plans or decisions have you been postponing waiting for the perfect time? What does the perfect time look like? What steps can you take individually and as a couple to move forward with one of your plans?

15
Busted Knuckles

Laura – I despise broke things. Wayne's mechanical savvy was a plus in our relationship.

I owned a white Chevy Citation when we met. Wayne detested my vehicle because it was always in need of repair and he was tired of busting his knuckles to fix its many ailments. After about a year of getting to know my vehicle in more ways than he wanted, he surprised me and bought me a car, using the money he was saving for the "any color but brown" van he had always dreamed of owning. This was BEFORE we got married, with no strings attached. Even if we didn't get married, the car would still be mine. Of course, my heartstrings were already attached, but this sealed the deal.

Wayne – I am still trying to decide if it was out of love or necessity. Yes, it's true I'm quite comfortable fixing things. My day job was to perform maintenance on gas engines, diesel engines, hydraulic equipment, and electrical equipment.

At first, fixing Laura's broken-down Citation made me feel like Fix-it Man. Note the words "at first." Her car would break down or not start at least once a week. It would never break down close to home. It was a mandatory 10 to 15-mile trek to get to the repair site. As the weeks continued, it became clear I needed to make a decision - continue my role as a maintenance man or expand my role into vehicle financer. I chose the latter.

My decision allowed my knuckles to mend at last, and I still felt like Fix-It Man, just in a different way.

#OurShade – With Wayne being willing to sacrifice the desire of his heart to give me the desires of my heart, we each knew we were in it together and definitely worth keeping.

#YourShade – When was the last time you made a conscious decision to sacrifice your wants to be a blessing to your spouse? How did it make you feel? When has your spouse sacrificed their desires to be a blessing to you? What was your response?

16
Runaway Bride

Wedding-day anxiety can happen to anyone, even when you are not the one getting married.

Laura – Here we are, 18 months after that initial rejection, awkward first dance, and crazy first date. Our big day has finally arrived. It was a sunny winter day in January of 1992, but Northern California winters are mild and even pleasant on most days. On this day, an evening rainstorm was in the forecast. The timing of the storm coincided with the time of our wedding. I was hoping it wasn't an omen about our marriage.

My Maid of Honor, Pat, and I were heading back to Beale AFB after a relaxing day at the hair and nails salons. I decided to take the back route to the base which was a two-lane highway that would take you straight toward Southern California. But instead of heading onto the base, I passed the entrance gate without slowing down. Pat looked at me warily.

"Laura, where are you going?"

I remained silent and kept my gaze locked on the road ahead of us. We soon approached another sign announcing an entrance into the base. I silently sped past that one also. My friend was growing increasingly anxious.

"La La, what are you doing?!"

I matched her franticness with my response.

"Pat, I just can't go through with this. If we stay on this road, we can head to Sacramento and just come back tomorrow."

She was in full panic mode by this time.

"Laura, no, we have to get to the church. I have to get you to the church. I am responsible for you!"

I increased my speed and Pat went into panic and anger overdrive as if thinking, how dare I put her in this position?

"Laura, turn around now. I mean it!"

Silence.

"LAURA! Turn this car around now!"

By this time, Pat's face was wet with shiny slivers of tears. You would have thought it was her wedding I was speeding us away from!

"Laura, that's it. Stop and let me out of this (insert a few choice words here) car. I can't face Wayne AND his mamma if you run away!"

She was so resolute in her stance that she tried to open the door while I was driving. What she did not know was, there was a little-used third entrance to the base that would put us closer to our destination. I didn't feel the need to give her the heads up about this. Since I was feeling playful and little mischievous, it seemed more, um, "fun" to let her come to the revelation on her own.

When we approached the last sign announcing the entrance to the base, I broke my silence and started laughing wildly. Poor Pat, meanwhile, was wiping away tears and breathing heavily, trying to choke back sobs.

It took her a while to get over that moment, and we still joke about the prank 26 years later. She promised to repay me for that stunt. I am still waiting, Pat!

#OurShade – When we invited people into our marriage, including our wedding party members, we chose those who saw our relationship as something valuable and worth protecting. Our friend, Pat, believed in our marriage, even before it started, so much so that she wasn't going to be a part of anything that would harm its success. She was indeed a Maid of Honor!

#YourShade – Who have you surrounded your relationship with that honor and respect it and are willing to help you protect it if ever think about "running away" from it? Take some time to thank them for their support and commitment. If they live near you, consider hosting a dinner to say thank you.

17
Graveyard Gratitude

"What a man…what a mighty good man" - Salt-N-Pepa

Laura – What is marriage without some cemetery shenanigans? Wayne didn't meet my family until AFTER we were married (sucka!). We were married in January of 1992 and took our first family road trip to Toledo, Oh in the summer of 1992. He then understood why our height difference was not an issue for me because my dad was about 1/2 inch shorter than Wayne. My height comes from my mom who was much taller than my dad.

During our trip, Wayne and I went to visit my mother's grave site, accompanied by our children, my sister, my brother, and my father. My brother, who is a minister, wanted to pray before we left the cemetery. Before he could open his mouth to pray, my sister dropped to her knees, lifted her hands and, because she was hearing impaired and wanted to hear herself, began to pray—loudly! This was a shock to me since I had never seen her pray and didn't know her to be a person of prayer. My brother and dad gave me a look that indicated they were just as shocked as I was. We just closed our eyes and went along with it. This initial shock was minor compared to the shocking prayer she offered….

"Momma, I thank God, Nay Nay (my nickname) finally brought a good man home!"

She said it with so much passion (and volume) I fully expected my momma to jump out of the grave and give my sister a high-five!

My eyes popped open in disbelief. I don't know if embarrassment is a strong enough word to use to describe my feelings. If there was an open grave nearby, I might have considered jumping in it! I could see Wayne and our children out of the corner of my eyes, holding back laughter while giving each other side-glances.

As the flush of embarrassment passed, I thought about the scene later, and I realized she was right. It made me even more appreciative of Wayne, knowing it was so obvious to others that I was blessed with such "a mighty good man."

Wayne – How can I best describe Laura's family? They were more like Sanford and Son rather than The Huxtables, and I fit in like a missing puzzle piece. Laura's dad, Clifford Bester Sr., was as cool as the flip-side of a pillow. He was a quiet man who welcomed me with open arms, (and one time with a clenched fist, but that's another story). If I had two words to describe Cliff, it would be the words Denzel Washington used in *American Gangster*, "My Man."

I must admit the cemetery scene was unexpected. I've received many accolades in my day; however, I can honestly say no one had praised God for me like that before or since then. I've been to many churches and seen a lot of "extra" during a service, but Laura's sister, Sharon, beat them all. After all of that, I had no choice but to hang in there with Laura. Sharon recently passed away, and there is now a gaping hole in my cheering section.

#OurShade – We can be guilty of taking our spouses for granted. Sometimes we need to view each other through fresh eyes to remind us of the extraordinary value the other brings the marriage.

#YourShade – Get a blank sheet of paper and in a vertical line write the letters of the alphabet, A-Z. For each letter, write a word or phrase of affirmation or appreciation about your spouse. Some things you can do with this list are:
- Put it in an envelope or card and give/mail it to your spouse
- Write a poem, song, or rap.
- Send one text a day praising them using a word from your list.
- Give them 26 kisses and repeat a word after each kiss.

Make up your own and send us your ideas!

18
Non-fatal Attraction

Honesty is always the best policy...or is it?

Wayne – Candy Burton (no, that's not her real name!) worked in the same area of the base as I did, teaching airmen in the maintenance area. Now, as any husband would do, I'd come home each evening to my lovely wife and talk about my day. That seems normal, right? I'd talk about the students that came to my classes, and the silly things my coworkers would say and do. However, I guess I mentioned one coworker too many times, or maybe it was the way I said her name, I don't know. What I do know is Laura started keeping track of how many times I mentioned my coworker Candy. Then one day, unexpectedly she asked,

"Are you attracted to Candy?"

WHAT??? If I didn't take care of this and answer "No!"

instantly, it was because I was taken completely by surprise. This was a defining moment in our relationship. I knew it was vital to get this right and didn't cause a problem by saying the wrong thing. I thought about using a car analogy, such as "Cadillacs are nice cars. I like the way they look, but I don't want to buy one". BAD CHOICE, Wayne. While I didn't want to buy a Cadillac, I'd love to take one for a ride. Who wouldn't? Therefore, no analogies. What should a man do in that situation? I'll let Laura take it from here.

Laura – Let's be honest, ladies, most of us know when something is amiss. We were barely into our first year of marriage when this happened, so my "wife antennas" were highly tuned. The first few times he mentioned Candy I was okay. After a few more days and weeks of hearing about how great Candy was at her job, how she has it all together, blah blah blah, alarms resounded in my head like the robot on the 1960 TV show *Lost in Space*, who would warn his human family of impending danger by frantically shouting "Danger, Will Robinson." My history of fear, jealousy, and insecurity tried to take control of my thoughts. Even then, I kept quiet because I didn't want to jump to conclusions. I decided Candy must be my enemy, and I wanted to know what I was up against.

My opportunity came at Wayne's workplace Thanksgiving party. We arrived early because he was responsible for setting up the location for the arrival of the guest and food. He made sure the tables and chairs were in place, and the space for the food was ready to receive its bounty. Candy was assigned to bring the turkey, but she was late, and my curiosity about her continued to grow. I know the turkey is the star of most Thanksgiving feasts, but you would have thought the president had gone missing, the way he was concerned about her tardiness. When Candy (and the turkey) finally arrived, I'll admit, she was pretty, petite, and had a beautiful smile, all the things high on Wayne's checklist. Going into stealth mode, I watched my enemy's interaction with my husband. To my surprise and relief, I realized it was a one-sided fascination.

The next day, I decided to pull the sheets off the whole thing and ask Wayne if he was attracted to her. His brief pause confirmed my hunch. His unwillingness to quickly deny or deflect my suspicions was answer enough. He was honest enough to confirm with a soft and guarded "Uh, I don't know, maybe."

You might think that bothered me. Well, it did, initially. But I was also impressed with his attempt at honesty and made it a point to reassure him it was understandable. Candy was pretty, had an infectious smile, and seemed like a nice person. I didn't yell, pout, cry or make him feel guilty about it. We talked it out and moved on. In fact, Candy and I became good friends, and we keep in touch on Facebook.

#OurShade – We are proud we were brave enough to tackle uncomfortable situations and conversations. We always expect each other to be honest enough to own up to our part, too. Even when things get shaken up a little, the dust settles eventually. When that happens, we reaffirm our love and commitment to the relationship we have built together.

#YourShade – What difficult conversation have you and/or your spouse been avoiding? Why have you been avoiding it?

19
Man Down, Thumbs Up

Wayne – As a maintenance instructor at Beale AFB, I had a great work environment. There were 15 instructors, and we went on different outings together with our families at least once a year.

In 1993, we took a weekend and went camping at a park near the base. We stayed up all night roasting a pig while our kids played. The next day my supervisor took some of us out on his boat. A couple of the instructors were good at water skiing. I wasn't one of them. But I was willing to try, and they were more than willing to teach me. Let me stop here and confess–I didn't know how to swim.

Anyway, I strapped the skis on my feet and jumped into the water. I popped up on my skis for about five seconds, and I fell. After three unsuccessful tries, we decided I should try tubing. That seemed easier than water skiing. At least, I didn't have to worry about keeping my balance. All I had to do was hold on to the straps attached to the tube. Like I said, easy.

The boat took off, and the ride is going smoothly. I was thinking, "Maybe I'm good at this after all."

That's when my supervisor decided to spice things up a

little. He turned the boat, and I flew over a wake. The inner-tube leaped out of the water, and I was airborne for several seconds.

Laura – I was reluctant to get on the boat during this trip. I knew neither one of us could swim. I took a precaution and made sure my lifejacket was secure before I hopped on the boat. Even then, it was despite my fear of water.

Imagine my chagrin when "Mr. I'll Try Anything Once" wanted to try water skiing. After the failed attempts I was relieved, thinking Wayne had satisfied his need for adventure, but my relief was only momentary since he decided to try tubing. After all, it's the same thing as the water skiing, except with a big inflatable tire instead of skis (so he thought). I watched with concern as my husband, who couldn't swim, secured his wrist in the straps, and waved at me with a cheesy grin. Our friend, Candy, was standing next to me and she was concerned too. Candy and I shared a temporary moment of silent panic when the tube went airborne then flipped over, and Wayne vanished. I tried not to let myself think the worst, but it was difficult because I was helpless at that moment. Even if Wayne needed my help in the water, there was nothing I could do to help.

Wayne – When the tube came down from its brief flight, I was upside-down with the tube on top. I remember feeling my head smack the water, then the tube, then the water, then the tube. The tube and I were bouncing along behind the boat. Finally, I don't know how it happened, but the tube flipped, and I was back on top. What could I do? I gave everyone the thumbs up and continued the ride.

Laura – It felt like the seconds stretched into minutes before the tube flipped back over and his face, with clenched teeth and squinted eyes, reappeared to give us the thumbs up. I was relieved, and a bit angry he would put himself in danger. I also made it a point from that moment to make sure his life insurance is always up to date!

#OurShade – There are times when one of us makes a decision the other doesn't agree with, and there's always the possibility the situation could go wrong. In this case, I (Laura) knew I would not be able to jump in and fix it. All I could do was the difficult thing–keep silent.

We have learned that when one of us won't listen to reason, it's best to practice silence and ask God to speak to both of our hearts about the decision, then step back, and trust God in the process.

#YourShade – How do you respond when your spouse makes a decision you don't agree with or understand? What do you do when your spouse disagrees with a decision you make? How can you show your support and trust even when you don't agree with a decision?

Challenge

List some family decisions that you are facing. Discuss possible outcomes if handled like a dictatorship (one person makes the decision without regard to other person's thoughts) versus a collaboration.

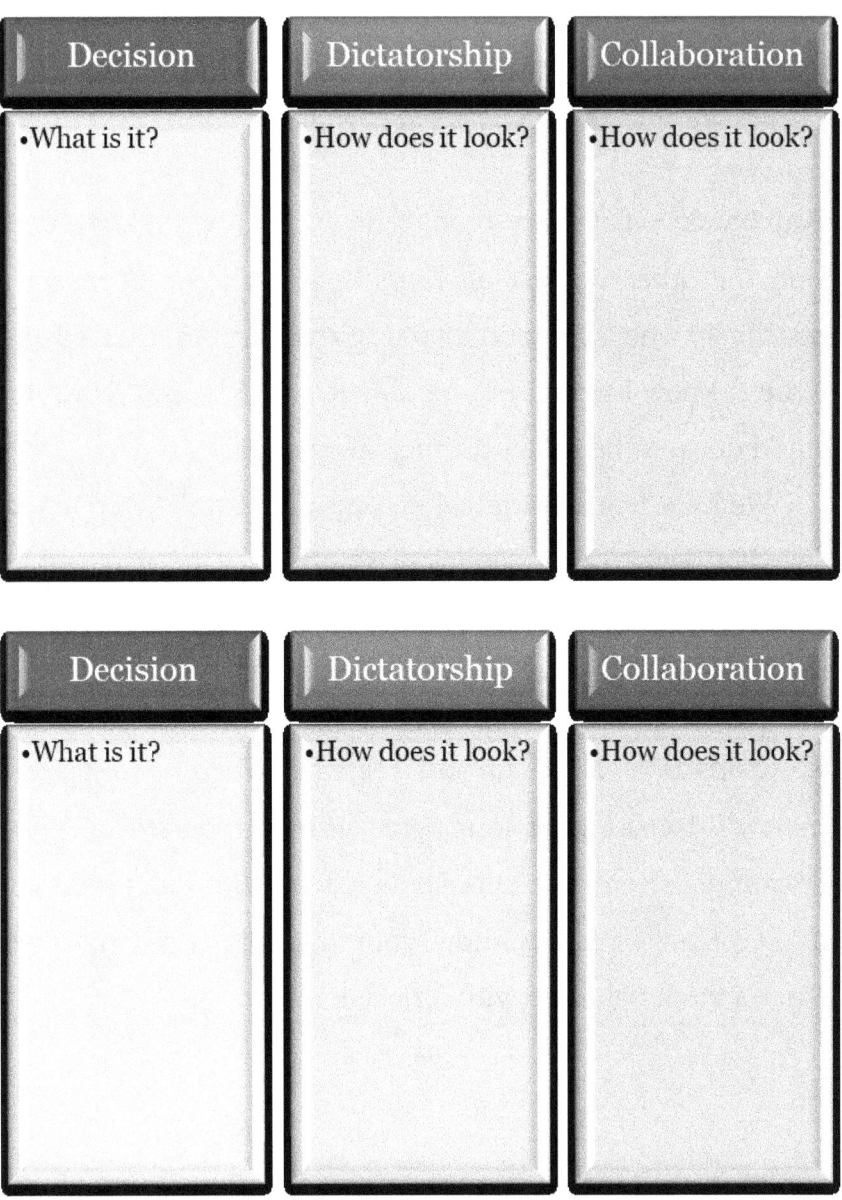

20
Indecent Proposal

Wayne – In 1993, The Black Heritage Committee on Beale AFB put on a live variety show. It was based on the "In Living Color" show hosted by Kenan Wayans. The monies raised from tickets were used to fund community events and activities for the year, such as picnics, and Poetry and Jazz nights.

The variety show had comedians (wannabe), dancers, poets, and anyone who wanted to share their talent. However, there was one requirement, you must audition. The audition was simple. Show your talent, and we figured out where to put it in the show.

Everyone practiced for days on end. This was our first time doing a production this large, and everyone was excited. The day of the show arrived. I was the emcee, so it was my job to keep the crowd engaged and keep the show moving. I guess I was doing a good job, at least that's what many people told me. Laura had a segment in the show where she delivered a "stop what you're doing" performance of her poem, *Understand Black Man*. I watched in awe because I had not seen this side of her. I was even more proud when the crowd gave a standing ovation.

Later in the show, I was sitting on the main floor off to

the side of the stage waiting to go back on stage to keep the crowd engaged between performances. Laura was backstage because she had another appearance in the show. To my surprise, this young lady, who was on the committee with us, came and sat next to me. She sat so close that our backs connected with only a tiny sliver of air between them. Although she made no verbal proposal, I wasn't that long out of the game that I couldn't understand implied intent. I could feel the old dog in me arise. What should I do? Test the waters and see if it meant anything? Get up and walk away quickly as if I couldn't handle the situation? Or somewhere in between? Oh, by the way, she was the type of young lady I would try to talk to—short, friendly, and... you get the picture.

Wisely, I chose the "somewhere in between" option. I didn't test the waters, but I didn't remove myself from the situation, either. I asked her if she was enjoying the show, she responded, and I got up and, strolled away and found somewhere else to sit.

Laura – Wayne did not tell me this happened until about fifteen years later. I feigned anger at him for not telling me sooner, but I was actually impressed with how he handled himself with integrity despite the culture we were a part of which condoned this behavior. He could have easily chosen to explore his options with her, and others would have covered for him. I know this because we watched it happen with other couples. There were a few young ladies in the group I kept my eyes on because, in my opinion, they laughed a little too hard and about 20 seconds too long at Wayne's jokes. He's a funny guy, but he's not that funny.

I often wonder how I would have responded had he told me the whole story back then. We hadn't been married for very long, and I was still struggling with confidence issues. Honestly, my maturity level in handling jealousy was not impressive. It would have been stirred up every time I saw her. There were other events and meetings we were involved in, and this young lady was a part of them. I know it would have changed the dynamics of my interaction with her and it would have changed the atmosphere of our meetings and events for everyone, not just for Wayne and me.

#OurShade – It is such a relief and sense of peace to know we can trust each other unconditionally. It takes work to build that level of trust, but it is worth it. Understanding who we are and what we like does not make us immune to temptation, but it does help to put temptation in its proper place. Who we truly are shows in our actions.

#YourShade – When should you tell your spouse when someone else flirts with you? How do you handle knowing someone is flirting with your spouse?

21
A Man is Just Gonna be a Man

Wayne

"A Man is gonna be a Man." For years, this statement has been used to justify fecal behavior. When you hear a woman say it, it's a guarantee some man has missed the mark by a long shot. I am grateful my father never modeled the type of behavior that would cause my mother to use this statement to mask her pisstivity (I know it's not a real word, but it should be) from an indiscretion.

One weekend, I went out to the club with the fellas from the Black Heritage Committee. As I look back, the character of some of the fellas was highly questionable. Nevertheless, Laura gave me a pass to go with them. Please note, only a few months prior, I was one the fellas. Therefore, I was wondering if this one of those tests to see if I would be faithful.

We arrived at the club, and there were ladies all over the place. It may not have been as many as I thought. However, when you know you can only dance and talk, it seems like there is more perceived temptation than actual temptation. In other words, when you worry about a thing, you start seeing it everywhere, even places it isn't. This time around, I felt like a Teflon Don. Every wink or "Heyyyy" didn't stick and pull me in. I had a great time because I knew no one at the club could compare to the one at home, not even for one night.

I made it back home with no lipstick stains, no phone numbers, and no reason to lie. I can't say the same for all the men that night. In fact, around 4:00 am, the phone rings and Laura answered it. It's the wife of one the guys. She asked Laura if I'm home or if I'm still out. You know that meant her husband hadn't made it home yet. I guess "A Man is Just Gonna Be a Man."

#OurShade – Opportunities to embarrass each other sometimes come our way. Our actions should give each other pride and ensure we never have to make excuses for each other's behavior.

#YourShade – What would cause you or your spouse to be embarrassed or feel a need to make excuses for the other's behavior? What steps can you take to prevent this from happening? (use another sheet of paper if needed.)

This would cause embarrassment	Prevention Steps

22
Don't Ask, Don't Tell?

Laura – While we are on the topic of temptation and wandering eyes and hearts, let's be clear and realistic, opportunities for temptation and infidelity will come. There is no magic wand or secret bubble you wrap your spouse or yourself in to prevent it. Even if you or your spouse looks like the back side of a baboon, there is someone who will find baboon-butt ugly, attractive. Can you handle that? The issue is not with temptation, it's with your response to it.

To be honest, Wayne and I have not had to face the issue of infidelity. I am not saying neither of one has been unfaithful. I am saying, to the best of our knowledge about each other, we haven't had to have the infidelity conversation. We have discussed the "what ifs" of the possibilities. And although we can harmoniously agree to disagree, we fall on separate sides of the fence when it comes to confessions of infidelity.

My thought is, if I don't know, then don't tell me. If Wayne had an affair years ago, and it slipped by me, then let it go! If he feels like he just needs to confess and get it off his conscience, he should find a priest, go to confessions.com, or write a letter and mail it to some fictitious location. Whatever just don't ruin my "happy place." You may call it naïve, or avoidance, but I call it being honest about myself and keeping my sanity.

Wayne, on the other side of the fence, says he'd want to know!

Wayne – Darn skippy, I want to know! If knowledge is power, then I want to be as strong as possible. Choosing not to tell me only works if nothing is ever discovered. The second that happens, I go down a rabbit hole. I start wondering, "What else have you been hiding?", "Why were you dishonest?", "You don't think I could handle knowing the truth?" The list would continue until my thought process would be so skewed, I would not be able to think straight.

So, please, please let me know ahead of time.

Laura – Well, I can guarantee he won't hear it from me. We also discussed what our responses might be if faced with the knowledge of our spouse's infidelity. Inquiring minds want to know? Both of us believe we would stay and work it out. Now, let me explain this before anybody starts to question our sanity. Had you asked us this question, "Would you stay?" in the first few years of our marriage, our answer would be "peace, I'm out!" But after we've invested 28 years of our lives into this relationship, we don't think we would want to toss it over someone's "15 minutes of fame". It would be difficult, but we both believe what we have built is worth the fight.

If you are facing the pain of adultery in your marriage, please know, it doesn't have to be the end! Although I can't decide for you, I can say, whatever decision you make, pray for God's wisdom first. Both of you must submit to wise and godly counseling. Also, whether you decide to stay or leave, you must choose to humbly walk in the power of forgiveness.

Of course, the best choice in any relationship is to remain faithful. If you are considering "coloring on a different canvas" we advise you to stop and think about the consequences. Think about your spouse. Think about your family. Adultery, even if it's never discovered changes the dynamics of people and of things. It changes how your spouse sees you, and it changes how you see yourself. Talk with a trusted friend, talk to your spouse about your feelings (scary, I know), and most importantly, talk to God! Do whatever it takes to keep you from dipping your brush in someone else's paint.

Although we haven't faced that choice in our marriage, we are familiar with the impact of infidelity (as victims and perpetrators) from past relationships. We understand the deep roots of anger and the bite of bitterness. It wasn't until we could forgive the other person and ourselves that we were able to move forward and be free of the weight of guilt, shame, and anger.

#OurShade – While fidelity is the best choice, we honestly accept that we may be presented with other options. We guard our hearts and minds in prayer. Praying that we may be able to choose wisely, so we don't embarrass our spouse, our families, ourselves, or God's name.

#YourShade – What would you do if faced with the truth of your spouse's infidelity? Would you leave? Would you forgive and stay to work on rebuilding trust? Would you stay and hold on to bitterness and anger? Choose wisely. Be brave, have the conversation about:

- **Attention** – How to handle sexual attention from others.
- **Prevention** – How to limit situations that give you an opportunity to be unfaithful.
- **Reconstruction** – How to handle the "what ifs."

23
The Silence of the Fam

Flowers won't fix everything!

Laura – Wayne came home bearing a dozen beautiful red roses. He smiled ever so lovingly and placed the roses in my arms... then handed me our orders to Germany. I was devastated. I didn't want to leave California. Yes, I knew we were a military family, yet it didn't make the news any easier to accept. I have never been one to like changes or handle them well, especially if I wasn't the one orchestrating the change.

And I wasn't the only one devastated by this news. The kids were heartbroken at the thought of leaving friends and starting a new school in a different country. All Air Force members must keep an updated assignment location request sheet. While this doesn't guarantee you get exactly what you want, it does help the Air Force keep your desires in mind when deciding location changes. I didn't recall Germany, or any overseas location, being on his assignment request sheet. A few days later I asked him when he changed his sheet. That's when he confessed he made the change and requested a move several months before he received the news of the new assignment. I was angry he didn't at least discuss this decision with me or give me fair warning that a massive change in our lifestyle was imminent.

My anger and sadness brewed. Our departure was set for December 1993. Since we had a few months before we had to leave, I hoped I would warm up to the idea, but watching the movers come and pack our stuff and take it away only made it worse.

We planned to drive to the east coast to visit our families in Ohio and Georgia before flying to Germany. When the day finally arrived to leave, the family barely helped Wayne pack the rest of our belongings. We purposely dawdled and disregarded his desires to leave early in the morning. I even made up some last-minute shopping trip. This caused his anger to intermingle with our anger.

The entire family gave him the silent treatment as we left California to head to Ohio to visit my family first (petty, I know). I think we loosened the grip on our lips 1500 miles later, somewhere around Nebraska.

Now, whenever Wayne brings me flowers, my first response is, "Are we moving?"

Wayne – The flowers were a failed attempt to lighten the moment. Laura was not a person who loved moving, even though she knew moving is a part of military life.

By the time I made the request for the transfer, I had

been stationed at the California base for almost six years. In my job, staying at the same base for more than four years is like a death wish for your career. I might have moved sooner if it weren't for meeting Laura and taking time to build a life with her.

In my mind, the pros of this move overwhelmingly outweighed the cons. In Laura's mind, and in the kids' minds, moving was the worst thing ever. This led to me getting minimal help packing for the trip. Imagine wanting to leave at a specific time, and NOBODY had their things packed. Thus, it became another one of those expletive-filled-bubble moments while I tried to get everything ready. We finally got in the car and headed for the east coast. Along the way, nobody talked to me. In their opinions, this whole unhappy experience was because of me. Even though I wasn't happy about having to do all the last-minute work, I understood the silence. The jury is still out on what was better, the silence or the usual back-seat arguments between the kids?

#OurShade – This is an example of the WRONG way to make a family decision and the WRONG way to respond to a decision or change we didn't agree with or understand. I could have given Laura and the kids the opportunity to weigh in on the decision. Marriage is a collaboration, not a dictatorship.

Since the decision and resulting orders were a done

deal by the time the family heard about it, it became my (Laura) job to show my support.

My actions and attitude affected our children's attitudes also. It was unfair to Wayne to make him feel guilty for wanting to advance his career to support our family.

#YourShade – When have you responded in a negative way to your spouse about something you disagreed with or didn't understand? Do you owe your spouse an apology?

If you need help with navigating change, contact us about our workshop
"S.H.I.F.T. Happens – Creative Strategies to Master Change"

Ramstein Air Base, Germany 1994-1998

24
Burnt Cookies & Scorched Feelings

Laura – Our first legitimate argument was over burnt cookies, in January of 1994. We were living in a small temporary lodging apartment, better known as TLF, shortly after arriving in Germany. When I say small, I mean it only had two bedrooms to house five people! This was a whopping (and unwelcome) change from our four-bedroom, split-level home we left in California.

I decided to try to cheer up my family and bring a little normalcy to the situation by making chocolate chip cookies for the family. After slaving over the package of Pillsbury cookie dough and lovingly slicing each cookie to uniform perfection, I put the cookies in the oven, set the timer, and went into our bedroom. Since the TLF was Lilliputian (yes, it felt that small to me), it meant I wasn't that far away from the oven. However, when the timer went off, I didn't hear it. Ten minutes later, I recognized the smell of burnt cookies wafting into the room. I dashed into the kitchen to investigate and notice the cookies were STILL in the oven…STILL cooking. After I pulled the "slightly overdone" cookies out of the over, I looked around and saw the family just sitting and watching TV as if the place didn't smell like an aftermath of a bakery fire.

"Wayne, did the timer go off?"

"Yeah."

"Did you smell the cookies burning?"

Unbothered, Wayne responds, "Yeah."

"Is there a reason you didn't take the cookies out or at least let me know they were done?"

The kids must have felt the tension brewing between Wayne and I (or maybe our raised voices gave them a clue) because they turned and shot a cautious glance at us and then at each other. The tension was a spill-over from my resistance to leave California and move to Germany (in the middle of winter—and have you ever experienced a winter in Germany?! It's a little bit colder than California). On top of that, there were five of us trapped in a small apartment while we searched relentlessly for a larger, permanent place to live in Germany.

Wayne offered his defense.

"Why did you set the timer and walk away if you knew you wouldn't be able to hear it from the other room?"

Really, Bruh? A heated discussion ensued which left us both a bit scorched toward each other. This was the only time our children have ever heard us argue.

Side note, the unexpected benefit of this is when the oven timer goes off now, EVERYONE makes a point to tell me, even the grandbabies!

Wayne – Out of all the things we had experienced together, we never argued. We would disagree on things and have different opinions, but we never argued. So why was the first argument about something as trivial as burnt cookies? I think the burnt cookies were the last straw. Laura and the kids were still a little miffed with me. We were a family of five, living in a two-bedroom temporary lodging facility, in a foreign country, halfway around the world from they wanted to be. Everything was in place for the first argument. I'm just glad we can joke about it.

Laura – Tension, anxiety, frustration, and other events beyond our control caused us to react to minor offenses with unreasonable behavior. Now, we always remind ourselves that our responses have the power to create chaos or calm. We both failed that day! But we do our best to choose wisely.

Before sharing the "shades" with you, we want to share a few more examples with you, because we think it's vitally important to know how to bring peace and calm into those chaotic storms and tense moments that will arise in any marriage.

Part I - Flame Thrower

For we wrestle not against flesh and blood, but against principalities, against powers, against the rulers of the darkness of this world, against spiritual wickedness in high places.
(Ephesians 6:12)

Laura - I know what the scripture says! I am honest enough to admit that despite that understanding, there were times I wanted to wrestle with the flesh AND draw blood. One such time was when Tasha was about ten years old. She had a friend named Jeanie at the house for a sleepover. They were self-sufficient and didn't need much attention beyond pizza, soda, and some music.

We were living in a three-level home in Germany, and we had been in the country for about a year. The bedrooms were on the second level, and the living area was on the third level. Tasha and Jeanie were in her room and Wayne, and I were in the living room. I am not sure where Ouidii and Real were at that moment, but they were innocent in this debacle. I started to smell something. I sniffed the air, looked at Wayne, and said,

"You smell smoke?"

Wayne sniffed.

"No."

I jumped up, ran down the steps toward the bedrooms, still sniffing.

"You don't smell that?"

A light cloud of bluish smoke was wafting in the hallway where the bedrooms were. Was my mind was playing tricks on me, I wondered?

"Do you see the smoke?"

This time Wayne nodded, and he opened Tasha's bedroom door. Her room was full of smoke, but even worse, the curtains were ablaze. Wayne rushed to snatch the curtains from the rods and stamped out the flames. Only after the immediate danger passed, we noticed Tasha and Jeanie standing there, frozen with confusion and fear.

When Wayne is angry, his nostrils will widen enough that you could hide a large marble in them. His nose will spread across his face as if an invisible hand is behind his head yanking his skin into a taut bow. He also does this harsh chuckle that sounds like a car trying to start, "heh, heh, heh."

Wayne asked, "What is going on in here?"

My concern turned to anger when I heard her explanation.

"We made a flamethrower."

Wayne gave the spread-nosed, "heh, heh, heh."

I thought I must not have heard her correctly.

"A what?" I asked.

That's when I noticed a lighter and a can of hairspray in her hand, and I understood what they did. They sprayed the hairspray in the air then fired up the lighter. The highly flammable aerosol created a flame when it came in contact with the fire from the lighter. Upon further inquiry, they admitted they had done this a few times before the curtains caught fire.

I was speechless as I surveyed the smoke still wafting in the air mixed with ashes from the curtains. The window had even cracked from the intense heat of the blazing curtains.

I didn't realize the full depth of Wayne's nose-spreading power until that night. If his nose was any wider, we'd have to give him another face to hold it.

Wayne decided it was best to take Jeanie home right away, so he called her mom and explained the situation. When they left, I instructed Tasha to sit in her room while I sat and contemplated my response.

At this point, I was a newly-minted Christian. It had only been a few weeks since I raised my hand in Church, so I had no practice of prayer or recalling scripture to help me through my anger or guide my actions. I relied on what I knew… my flesh. I jumped up and dashed to her room and began gathering all her things (clothes, radio, dolls). I had no clue what I was going to do, but it seemed like a formidable action.

By this time Wayne returned and came into Tasha's room and sat on the bed in silence. I had another epiphany. I grabbed the hairspray and wildly sprayed Tasha's hair. A look of confusion and terror came on her face, and she stumbled backward into the small space between the wall and her dresser.

Feeling a bit like Evilene, from "The Wiz," I said, "So, you like starting fires, do you?"

I grabbed the lighter, and her confusion turned to fear. I angrily flicked the wheel of the lighter until I was rewarded with fire. With arms stretched I pointed the flaming lighter in her direction and inched closer. By this time, she was screaming, and tears covered her face. The situation was spiraling out of control and might have had a dangerous outcome. Instead—

"Laura."

Wayne broke his silence with one word, spoken in a calm voice in stark contrast to the chaos before him.

That one word, my name, whispered in a tender and calm voice, rescued me from my delirium and brought relief to the hair-sprayed, teary-eyed child, trapped, and cowering on the floor. I dropped the lighter and marched into our bedroom. Feeling angry and defeated, I cried out "God, I need you to tell me something!"

I grabbed my NIV Bible, even though I was still clueless as what to look for. But I knew I had to look because anything would be better than what I was feeling. I opened it to a random page, and the words jumped out at me with clarity and assurance.

"In your anger do not sin, do not let the sun go down while you are still angry, and do not give the devil a foothold." (Eph. 4:26).

An indescribable calm washed over me. I returned to Tasha's room very different than the "Laura" who had left it a minute earlier. We talked peaceably even though I was still angry, and together we worked out a fitting punishment that did not include hairspray and fire.

This was a defining moment in my walk with Christ. Wayne was the still, small voice, calling my name, keeping me from foolishness. The word of God was the confirmation I needed to know He speaks through His word to those who are called by His name and are willing to listen.

To be clear, I wasn't really going to set her on fire. I wanted to scare her—mission accomplished—but I realized the foolishness of my actions. One small misstep could have meant, whoosh, girl on fire!

Of course, Wayne has had his moments also…

Part II - Date with a Baseball Bat

Wayne - This is a flash-forward to 2001 in North Carolina. We had teenagers in our home, and that brought countless moments of parent/child tension.

I love to watch "Animal Planet," especially the episodes with male animals battling for supremacy. Some behaviors are universal to all God's creatures, I suppose. Like many fathers and sons, Real and I had reached the point where he wanted to assert his budding manhood, and I wanted to insert my fully-formed foot in his butt.

One night the relationship hit a boiling point. Real was out with his friends and didn't come back home when he was supposed to. I called him to find out why he wasn't home. When he answered his phone, he used a casual tone with me as if he was talking to one of his friends.

"Son, do you know who you are talking to?"

His nonchalant and defiant response was,

"Yeah."

By this time the old bull was only seeing red. I told him he needed to get his ASSets home, and quickly! I hung up the phone and decided the young bull must be taught a lesson or slaughtered.

According to Laura, I grabbed a baseball bat and waited for him to return. I don't remember the baseball bat. That might sound like a joke, but it's not. It means I was so mad I blanked out some of that night. While I was sitting outside in a lawn chair, in ambush mode, Laura tried her best to calm me down by gently rubbing my head. It usually worked, but not that time. All I could think about was the most efficient, decisive way to take him down. The throat and the kneecaps seemed like good choices. Either way, it would be quick. Laura continued trying to be the calm. I don't remember what, if anything, she said. I do remember her quiet and calm presence.

As Real was riding the bike into the yard, I got up to meet him. For some reason, I didn't carry out my plot to disable the young bull (perhaps the head rub did work). I ended up grabbing him and forcefully letting him know that talking to me like a friend was not a wise idea for healthy living. A better idea would have been to answer with a simple and respectful "yes" or "no"... okay, scratch the "no."

Thanks to God's grace and Laura's calming spirit, the father-and-son-relationship is still intact, and the young bull lived to see another day.

Part III- Kicking Dad's Ass

Laura – Flashing back to 1992, Beale AFB, CA, there was a time in our marriage when I had no clue how to calm a storm.

All three children were in trouble one day. They were still learning how to bond in our new blended family. Each of them had this habit of treating their siblings like leftovers when they had friends over to the house. This day was no exception. Ouidii was mistreating the other two in favor of her visiting friend. Once this was brought to our attention, Wayne sent the friend home. Our kids then had to endure the usual extended talk, complete with drill-sergeant volume, then they were banished from Wayne's presence. They were collectively angry with him and went upstairs. Tasha went to her room, and Ouidii and Real tried to console each other. A little later, Real came downstairs and with all sincerity said he wanted to tell Wayne something.

"Dad, I have something to tell you."

Wayne wasn't in the mood for conversation with anyone in the house yet, and he gave Real the death stare.

"Yes, son?"

"I'm only telling you this in case you hear on the streets later."

"What is it, son?'

"Ouidii said she was so mad at you that she wanted to kick your ass!"

"Heh, heh, heh, is that right?"

Wayne called everyone together from the different corners of the house. He asked Oudii if Real was telling the truth. She was brave (or foolish) enough to say yes. This was the moment when Angry Dad from the Dark Abyss was unleashed. I won't tell you all the expletives that came out, but it ended with him threatening to kick everyone's ass, including their friends too.

I silently watched the peace of my household erode in less than an hour. At this time in our marriage, I did not understand I had the power of influence to calm the storm in my husband or my home. It took several hours for peace to return. No thanks to me!

#OurShade – There are times when one of us has emotions in overdrive. Sometimes we are the direct cause, and other times, it may have nothing to do with the other person. We've learned to activate our power of influence to bring peace into an angry or chaotic situation. In times of crisis, we want to be the calm and not the storm. It's good for more than that one person—everyone around can appreciate and benefit from it.

#YourShade – What can you do to calm the storm in your spouse and to calm your spouse in their storm? What is your plan to create calm versus chaos when facing conflict with your spouse? Take some time and discuss a "peace-keeping" plan. Include code words, phrases, or actions that could bring peace into each other's storm.

25
Soul Matters

Laura – Even though I didn't want to go to Germany, I am glad we did. Before we left California, since we weren't ready to commit to faithful church attendance, we decided to start going to Sunday School as a family. Wayne had grown up a church boy but had strayed (far, far away). I didn't grow up going to church on a regular basis (funerals and Easter don't count) or knowing much about the Lord. I guess something was stirring within both of us to get our family on a spiritual path.

In Germany, we decided to get serious about our family's spiritual growth. We started our spiritual walk with Christ together under the love and care of Chaplain (Rev.) Kevin Ivan Jones and his beautiful wife, Carla. We received a solid spiritual foundation and a shining example of ministry and marriage to build the rest of our lives upon.

Chaplain Jones called me a tabula rasa, meaning a blank slate, and I was indeed a blank slate when it came to the Bible. I have always been an eager learner, so I committed myself to attending weekly Bible study. Wayne did not go with me at first (he already knew everything… *right?*) but seeing my tenacity, hearing about what I learned, and refusing to be outdone by me, motivated him to attend regularly with me. This marked the beginning of our journey in Christ, together.

Wayne – No matter how far I strayed, the Word of God was always present. My family (immediate and extended) nurtured my love of God. While there were some things about God's representatives that disheartened me, God's love was always comforting.

When I returned to the church, I gained new insight into Proverbs 22:6. "Train up a child in the way he should go: and when he is old, he will not depart from it (KJV)," because it was always within me. Germany was the place I decided to accept God's love and his purpose for my life. Walking together with Laura was yet another example of God's love toward me.

#OurShade – Sometimes the thing we resist the hardest, is the thing we need the most.

#YourShade – What change are you resisting? What is the root of your resistance? List ten positive outcomes that could result from making this change?

26
Speedo Man

Oh, the joy of a fat man's crotch in your face, said no one, ever!

Wayne – During one of our yearly church retreats we were enjoying a day at an indoor pool resort called Hambachtal, in Germany. In addition to a large pool, there was a standing whirlpool in the middle and a slide. The whirlpool was a semi-circle shape. When the jets of the whirlpool started, it would push you around the path. However, if you were short (under 5' 6"), you could get sucked underwater. This meant it could be fun or it could be tricky. Laura, at 5' 7 ½", did well in the whirlpool.

The slide was a different story. It was one story tall with several curves. Laura was very reluctant to come down the slide. I convinced her to go by telling her we could slide down together. We climbed to the top and started our decent. Laura was in front, and I sat closely behind her. Every three feet, Laura would stop herself from going down too fast by sticking her arm and legs out against the slide. It took her a while to complete her seminal trek down the slide. Once she made it, she felt more confident.

Then, she decides to go solo.

I'm standing in another part of the pool when I turn to

watch her make it down the slide. She makes it down, splashes into the water, and stands victorious. Then, like watching a train wreck in slow motion, I see the human version of the titanic zooming down the slide, and I am powerless to stop the impending crash. Next thing I know... I'll let Laura tell the rest of it.

Laura – "Go down the slide, he said." "It will be fun," he said. "What's the worst that could happen?" he said. Well, it's all fun and games until a full pair of speedos hits you in the face!

After making my solo trek down the slide and feeling confident and accomplished, I took a moment to catch my breath. It was a short-lived victory.

I tried to regain my sense of direction and realized I had turned around and was now facing the slide. Yeah, I know that is a dangerous place to be! I struggled to move, but I was not quick enough. With the speed of greased lightning and the power of at least 300 lbs. of flesh on his side, a man, wearing speedos barely large enough to cover his man parts, came barreling down the slide. In what seemed like cinematic slow-motion, I stood squarely in the cross-hairs of his fast-approaching crotch. I watched, helpless and dumbfounded, as his crotch connected with my face (insert resounding wet, splashing, splatting sound effect here) ... SPLAT!

Down I went like Jonah into the depths of the pool.

Okay, I am dramatic, but it felt like an eternity before I came back up again. Remember, I can't swim, and I was never fond of the water. In his defense, the Speedo man looked equally shocked and discombobulated as he stopped to adjust his twisted man panties. After that ordeal, I exited the pool, and you might not be surprised to learn I did not get back in for the rest of our stay at the resort.

#OurShade – We don't want to get too comfortable after a success. It's important to stay on guard, because "Fat Man Life" wrapped in speedos may be right behind you!

#YourShade – List your personal and marital successes. How can you elevate those successes to the next level?

27
Downhill Screams

Wayne – Living in Germany gave us a chance for new experiences. The Alpine Slide was one of those experiences. A rider sits in a little cart on wheels and zooms down a narrow track, hundreds of feet long. Gravity propels the slide down the side of the mountain at tremendous speeds. The slide has a handbrake that helps the riders regulate the speed.

Because we do things together, Laura and I decided to ride in the same cart and made our way down the side of the mountain. I sat in front and Laura sat behind me, with her arm wrapped securely around my waist. I was a little more daring and wanted to feel the wind as we sped through the curves. I realized (later), Laura wanted a more conservative speed. The faster we went, the tighter she squeezed my waist and the louder she screamed, "LANGSAM!" Unfortunately, I didn't take the Conversational German class and didn't have a clue what she was saying.

Laura – Once again, I joined "Mr. I'll Try Anything Once" on a daring adventure. What's the worst that could happen going down the side of a mountain in a coaster seat just big enough for two, with nothing but a small handbrake to control the speed, right?

I trusted his judgment, so I suggested he ride in front

and control the speed. There were signs along sides of the track warning the riders to slow down when approaching curves. The signs were in German. I had taken a German course while attending the University of Maryland in Germany, so I understood the warnings. Unfortunately, Wayne did not.

As we approached the first langsam warning sign, which means SLOW, I noticed Wayne did not slow down.

"Langsam!" I screamed.

He didn't respond and sped right through the curve.

My heart was ready to leap out of my body when we approached another langsam sign. Once again, Wayne did not slow down, and I entered full-screaming-banshee mode.

"Laaaangsam, LANGSAAAAM!"

This happened once more, and by the end of the ride I was shaking, angry, and out of breath from all the screaming. I looked at him in wild-eyed disbelief and asked,

"Did you hear me screaming langsam!? Did you see all of those signs?"

"Yes, I heard you and saw the signs."

"Well, why didn't you slow down?"

"I didn't know what the signs meant, and I thought your screams meant you were enjoying the ride, so I kept doing what I was doing."

Bless his heart...

#OurShade – All communication is not effective. Talking and listening without mutual understanding leads to dangerous miscommunication.

#YourShade – When has there been a gap between what you or your spouse said, and what you understood? Do either of you say one thing but mean another? How can you avoid this in the future?

Try this:

Listen - To what your spouse is saying…

Repeat your interpretation - What I hear you saying is…

Confirm or correct - Yes, that's what I meant, or no, that's not what I meant.

Rephrase - Let me say it another way…

28
Uphill Battles

Usually, watching your husband touching another woman's butt is not funny. As you know by now, we are not your usual couple.

Laura – While on a winter church retreat in Austria, our group had to hike up a steep hill to get to a meeting location. Austrian winters are notoriously cold and icy, so the hill was slick and riddled with patches of ice. Some women, due to their lack of agility and abundance of, um… let's just say "ASSets," were having trouble getting up the hill without slipping and sliding downhill. They needed help!

Wayne, being the superhero, sprang into action. He placed himself behind some of the women and pushed them, one by one, as they struggled uphill (many times). One woman he helped was… uhm… how do I say this nicely? She was exceedingly blessed in the weight department. Wayne is 5'6" and maybe weighed 151 and one-half pounds… yeah, so you see where this is going.

Imagine, Wayne pushing this woman up the icy hill and the only way to get traction was by positioning his shoulder and hands under her butt and shoving her forth. She would slide back down a little bit taking Wayne with her, and each time, he would just lean in and shove harder.

Where was I during these heroics? I was off to the side of the hill between the trees, using the trees and snow for traction. I had a bird's-eye view of the show with Wayne and this ample woman as I was climbing and sometimes crawling uphill. My heart was full of admiration watching my husband so committed to helping this woman. And my face was wet with cold tears from laughing! Wayne was tired, sweaty, and a bit dazed by the end, but he survived. That was a whole new meaning of "leave no man (woman) behind."

Wayne – Thank God for the extra half pound. Without it, I would have been buried in the snow. The wonderful thing about that night was I was not the only guy trying to help the ladies up the hill. Several of us were slipping, sliding, and stumbling. We got to the point where it was just a comical experience. I'm sure the ladies we were helping felt a little embarrassed. They had to endure groping and squeezing in places reserved for their closest confidants. On the bright side, for the rest of our retreat, we were able to change the meeting location to another building that didn't involve climbing a hill!

#OurShade – Sometimes other people will need more of my spouse's attention than I do. We are willing to (temporarily) sacrifice our time together so we can be a blessing to someone else. It is essential we always remember to encourage each other in our willingness to uplift others in their time of need.

#YourShade – When has your spouse gone above and beyond to help others? Tell them how much you admire them for the sacrifice of their time to help others.

29
The Hole on My Butt

Laura – I don't do medical visits often, so when I do it's something that's really bothering me. Around the beginning of 1997, we were still living in Germany, when I noticed a growing lump on my (very) lower back. I had back surgery to remove a damaged disc several months before this, so I wanted to make sure all was well. The doctor examined the lump and, the next thing I knew, the doctor scheduled me for surgery in half an hour! It was a *sebaceous cyst. While it was not life-threatening, it called for immediate removal.

The cyst was the size of a cluster of grapes, and the incision and removal left a deep hole in that area. The doctor didn't add stitches because he wanted it to heal from inside… (there's a more profound message in that process, don't you think?). The doctor packed the hole with a medicated tape that needed daily changing. As timing would have it, we were heading into a three-day weekend which meant the clinic would be closed and I would have to go to the ER to have the dressing changed each day, unless… my

---

*Sebaceous cysts are noncancerous cysts of the skin… that may contain liquid or semiliquid material… www.healthline.com

husband was willing to come in and learn how to change it. Of course, Wayne, my hero, willingly obliged.

I have a high tolerance for pain, so when I tell you it hurts, believe me, it hurts! I had to lay on my stomach, and Wayne had to pull the medicated tape (along with any scarred flesh attached to it) out of the hole and then pack it with fresh medicated tape. The hole was deep, so he had to shove the tape down to fill it completely. I muffled the screams the best I could, but a pillow can only silence so much pain. At the same time, I felt terrible for him because it pained him to inflict so much pain on me. We endured this routine together for three days. How do you say thank you to your husband for packing your hole? Ah… never mind.

Wayne – The incision for the cyst was more on the lower back than being a hole on the butt. Nevertheless, it was excruciating for Laura. Imagine having to ask a husband who jokes about most everything, to take the old gauze packing out of the incision, then insert fresh gauze packing. I am proud to say I kept the jokes to a minimum. As her husband, I had to step up to the plate and do what was needed. That was not the time to be squeamish. Laura needed a pseudo-surgeon, and Dr. Brown was in the house. I'm glad she trusted me not to inflict any added pain.

#OurShade – Sometimes one of us may have to hurt the other (feelings, ego, ideas, etc.) to bring healing and wholeness to them. Through many trials and errors, we learned to give and receive sincere "tough love" in the process. This takes trust and patience because it is not always received well. We strive to have each other's best interest in mind even when it hurts

#YourShade – When it comes to your spouse, how well do you give or receive "tough love"?

30
The "BUT" in Our Lives

Laura – We had some wonderful adventures while we lived in Europe. There are too many to recount in detail, but I will give a short recap. We…

… spent the night in a German castle hotel— BUT we got lost along the way.

… visited to Disneyland in Paris—BUT got stuck on an indoor amusement ride and took a much-needed nap.

… hopped a train to Paris and visited the Louvre. I took a "shade" pic next to the famed Mona Lisa (BUT we realized she ain't all that).

… climbed the 284 stairs of the Arc de Triomphe to get a breathtaking (BUT out of breath) view of Paris.

…saw the beautiful cathedral of Notre Dame (BUT it was obscured by tons of construction scaffolding).

… we visited the Eiffel Tower (BUT only the outside). Why only the outside? The workers happened to be on strike that day, and we couldn't go inside! Years later and I am still salty about that!

Overall, living in Germany was good to us and good for us despite the BUTS.

Our next assignment to a new duty station was Seymour Johnson AFB in Goldsboro, NC. (Where the heck is that, right?!) When we first heard about it, we had to look it up online. Our search gave us some useful information about our new location, BUT the search also included "See More Johnson." An assembly line of pornographic and risqué images continued to pop on the screen. We were using Wayne's computer at work, and of course, everything you do online is subject to military review! It made me laugh to see Wayne frantically tapping on the keyboard trying to get out of these pictures.

Wayne – This was 1997. Use of the internet was really taking off. For the military, they were trying to get a handle on what was unauthorized use of the internet at work. Looking up information on a new assignment was an authorized use. Therefore, all things should have been in order. That was not the case since someone forgot to tell the search engine what was and was not authorized. Luckily, there were no repercussions or embarrassing calls from my superiors.

#OurShade – Every marriage, no matter how great, will have its "BUTS". Some will be big BUTS, some will be small BUTS. It's not the size of the BUTS that matter. We realized the important thing is how we handle BUTS when they smack us in the face. To avoid stinky attitudes, we spray our BUTS with grace and patience, and we insert a healthy enema of humor to keep our marriage fresh.

#YourShade – What are some BUTS in your marriage? How can you maintain a healthy attitude when faced with BUTS?

Seymour Johnson AFB, NC

1998-2005

31
Time-Share Take Down

Laura — After living on base for a year, we bought our first home in North Carolina in 1999, and that became the official start of the "Kool-Aid House." The urban dictionary defines Kool-Aid House as "The place where everyone wants to have fun and hang out, the cool house."

Our budget was limited, but our need was great. It was difficult finding a home with our wants that fit within our budget. We decided to take a small vacation break with the kids during the house hunt, and we signed up to take part in a timeshare "vacation" in Virginia. You know, the ones where they give you a free stay after you endure hours of marketing and strong-arm sales tactics. Of course, we had no intentions of buying a time-share, and we expressed that in many ways to the sales guy. I understand he has a job to do, but sometimes it goes too far. After hearing a bevy of nays from us, he decided it was time for the big guns in this war for our checkbook. He brought his boss in to try to convince us we were missing the deal of a lifetime.

As frustration mounted on both sides, we explained it wasn't the right time for us because we were house-hunting and need to be mindful of finances. We thought that would end the discussion. This super-sales guy begins to admonish us and even went so far to suggest our children would rather have a lifetime of two-week vacations per year versus a permanent place to call home. I heard the familiar "heh, heh, heh" from Wayne, and I knew, without even need to look at Wayne, the sales guy had just pulled the pin out of the grenade, and an explosion was imminent.

Wayne – As a husband and provider, I thought I was doing a pretty good job for my family. So, when this person tries to insinuate that our careful, family choices were depriving our children of great vacation experiences, I wanted to hit him in the soft part of his throat. Instead, I recounted to him the lifetime of memories our children already have, including Paris, Austria, Spain, and The Black Forest. Silence gripped his throat and humility snatched his tongue. The sales pitched abruptly ended.

Laura – We returned to NC and found our first home the next day, beginning a lifetime of memories. We are forever grateful for the lifelong friends who enjoyed our Kool-Aid home and became our family.

#OurShade – We won't allow others to force their dreams and desires on our relationship goals. We have our vision, and we make it plain. If others can't respect us… THEY NEED TO KEEP IT MOVIN'!

#YourShade – Do you have a clear and unwavering vision

for your marriage? Do you keep it written or visible anywhere in your home? Do you know how to articulate your vision to others?

The vision for our marriage and home is R.I.V.E.R. The word is displayed on our dining room wall so all who enter our home recognize the standard we have set for our home. It also serves as a reminder to us when we start to veer off track! It is large enough to be visible from the street when our curtains are open. We enjoy when people ask us about it because it gives us an opportunity to teach them how to create their own marital vision.

> **Contact us for more information about the "Create Your Marital Vision" workshop.**

32
Internet Mojo

Wayne – It's the late 90s, and the internet is steadily changing. This was when, if you were on the internet, no one could call you on the home phone. To solve that problem, you could set up an internet voice mailbox – problem solved.

During this time in our marriage, I was at a low point. Not at a Cialis low, but I knew I wasn't 21 (or 31 for that matter) anymore. One day I was doing some work on the internet. To encourage me, Laura left me a sexy voice message. Instead of checking my messages when I finished working, like I normally would do, I got up to do something else. Ouidii, our oldest daughter walked in after I left. She started surfing the web. Being more diligent than her father, she checked the messages. Imagine the look she had on her face when she heard the message. Unfortunately, she couldn't unhear the message.

Laura – I have had my share of embarrassing marriage moments, and this one ranks in the top five! I knew Wayne was going through a personal rough patch— at work, in ministry, and at home. It seemed no matter how many times I said, "It's okay," it never made him feel better.

"This called for a touch of creativity and spontaneity!" I thought.

Knowing he usually, USUALLY, checked the messages once he's done working on the computer, I had the brilliant idea to leave a... let's say... a very encouraging message, including some cutesy verbiage about his mojo still working just fine, which was from a line from the "Austin Powers - the Spy Who Shagged Me" movie. I wasn't paying attention to when he finished working on the computer.

All I do know is I heard howling laughter from the room where the computer was located. I was clueless what Wayne and our daughter were laughing at, and it didn't strike me as something to investigate. They laughed together on a regular basis. The laughter increased as Real and Tasha joined the room. Wayne finally came to get me, sporting a mischievous smirk on his face suggesting there was something amiss. I entered the computer room where all eyes turned to me, and our Ouidii wore the twin version of his smirk, and it hit me... awwwww man... she listened to the message! We all had a good laugh, at my expense. Wayne learned a valuable lesson about checking messages, and I learned never to leave risqué messages for my husband on the computer.

#OurShade – Although the intent to encourage was sincere, we learned technology is not a replacement for reality. Twitter, Instagram, and Facebook are fun, but real face time with each other is vital.

#YourShade – How much does technology affect communication in your marriage? How long can you sit with each other without looking at your phone?

Challenge – Next time you go out to dinner, plan to leave your phones in your purse, pocket, or (secure and hidden) in your vehicle. While waiting for your meal, engage in meaningful dialogue with each other. If you find conversation difficult, try this.

1. Create conversation starters on small slips of paper. This could be questions or thoughts that have been on your mind, but you never take the time to discuss them.

2. Play the "Memory Game". Each spouse takes a turn and recall a pleasant memory from the past and discuss how your memories differ.

3. This may be awkward at first, but it okay to just sit and hold hands instead of the phone.

You don't have to wait until you go out for dinner.
Try this at home too.

33
Sex-ish - The Naked Truth

As Good as I Once Was - Toby Keith

Wayne – As a young man, I would say I had a high libido, or that's what I thought I was supposed to have. When I turned 40, I realized I was 12 years removed from when I first met Laura. This period can bring many physical and psychological changes to a man, both good, and not so good.

After a full physical checkup in my 40th year, I received a clean bill of health. However, I noticed my energy level had decreased, and I was waking up tired. Additionally, I would run my annual 1.5 miles fitness run and be exhausted afterward. This had me worried because when my father was in his 60s, he was still climbing ladders and working on roofs. Surely, I should have been a chip off the old block.

All those physical issues were affecting our sexual relationship and intimacy. My mind is engaged like a 28-year-old, and my body was responding like a 40-plus-year-old who did the minimum to stay in shape. For me, this created frustrating scenarios in my mind.

"Does Laura notice?" I wondered." "Is she frustrated also? Is this a degenerative issue?" Each question led to another question, and I found myself down a dark rabbit hole.

I've heard the first Rule of Holes is when you find yourself in one, stop digging.

That's what I did, or so I thought when I went to the doctor to get a professional opinion. He gave me the information I already knew: aerobic activity (low or moderate workouts) would increase my endurance and overall health. Also, my diet needed more attention. I had reached the point where I couldn't eat any and everything I wanted to eat if I wanted to be healthy. That was too simple.

Next, I went online to do some research. That rabbit hole was wider and deeper than the one I created in my mind. I had to sort through natural and unnatural solutions. Lest I forget, there were a plethora of religious and supernatural solutions.

Lastly, I decided to ask Laura… what a brilliant idea! If anyone had insight on what I was going through, it would be her. She saw internal issues that eluded the doctors' examinations. She sensed my anxieties and frustration. The most wonderful thing is she also helped me find solutions. Once I put my pride aside and WORKED on the solutions, our relationship moved from stagnation to a higher level of intimacy.

Laura – Women are not immune to changes in sexual desires and abilities, especially as we mature; we just don't talk about them as much as men do. Work schedules, children, household responsibilities, and the natural changes in our beautiful female bodies work together to wreak havoc on sexual desires over the years. Also, a failure to take care of our physical health affects our sexual health.

Women tend to resist discussing sexual needs with our men—what we like and how things change. There is an often-quoted phrase that says, "What you did to get your spouse is the same thing you must do to keep them." In my twenties and thirties, I co-signed on that statement, nodding my head, and pursing my lips, "Hmm, hmm, yeah, that's right." But now, a more seasoned version of me calls a timeout on that statement. Why? Because time has a way of changing people.

I was 23 years old when I met Wayne. I am now in my fifties. What he did to get the 23-year-old, immature, self-conscious, jealous, and half-baked Laura is woefully inadequate for the mature, confident, purpose-driven, and a full-bag-of-chips, Laura. If he could do the same things and keep my attention, that shows a lack of growth on my part. If the same things I did to get the 28-year-old Wayne satisfies the 56-year old Wayne, then he has become stagnant in his growth.

Sexual changes, body changes, need, and desires are an evolving process in a long-term relationship. The key is to acknowledge, embrace, and most importantly, communicate those changes. Don't rely solely on fancy studies or surveys that asked 100 men/women what they want. Unless your spouse was one of those 100 people asked, the information is just that, information. I don't care what 100 men said they like. My concern is with the one I'm responsible for satisfying. I don't care if 51 ½ % of women enjoy a sexy spanking. If Wayne tried that, we'd have another story to put into this book!

#OurShade – Sexual desires and needs change over the course of a long and healthy marriage. Thank goodness we figured out how to check our egos at the door, put the surveys in the proper perspective, and have meaningful conversations about our needs. Discussing areas of change and dissatisfaction can be uncomfortable, and even tense at first. We understand that changes in our sexual needs are nuanced, natural, and necessary for growth. We keep the lines of communication open, and we stay willing to adjust to accommodate our changing needs. We haven't' always gotten it correct, but we are working on it.

#YourShade
Find a survey or study that discusses the sexual needs of men and women. Read it together.
1. On a blank sheet of paper, create three columns and number them from 1-10.
2. Label the first column "what the survey says my spouse wants/need."
3. Label the second column "what I think my spouse wants/need."

4. Label the third column "what my spouse says they want/need."
5. Fill out the first two columns on your own.
6. Discuss your answers with your spouse, then fill out the third column using insights from your discussion. Are there any surprises?

34
Running Stop Signs

Laura – while tasked with driving the women's dance ministry to and from an engagement, Wayne almost KILLED us. Okay, maybe I'm being dramatic, again.

It was past midnight, and the women were tired from working all day Friday, traveling to serve in ministry, and dancing, and sitting through a long church service, and we were all eager to get home. The road was lightless and narrow, and Wayne, who was just as tired, and eager to get home, was speeding down the road. I noticed a stop sign ahead, but he was not slowing down... I stayed silent because I thought "surely, he sees the sign." At the last possible minute, I spoke up, quietly and calmly (If you recall the Alpine Slide adventure in Germany, you already know yelling wildly doesn't help.).

"Baby, there's a stop sign..."

Wayne slammed on the brakes, the church van shimmied into a side swerve that threw the other ladies (who weren't wearing seatbelts) left and right into each other. He swiftly corrected it, took us out of danger, and brought the van to a screeching halt. There were ear-shattering screams, pounding hearts, and more than a few beads of sweat dropped that night. The women's dance team made it back home safely to dance another day. They also remembered to always wear their seat belts when Wayne was driving!

Wayne – It seems I was always the designated van driver. Part of that status is because I love to drive. Driving means I am in control. Most of the people in the ministry had no problem with letting me drive. Many times, our ministry events would last into the late hours of the night, and I was usually a perfectly safe driver.

On this night, we went to a church in a rural area with no street lights, just country roads. I remember seeing the stop sign; however, it looked as though the sign was for the crossing traffic only. I also remember hearing Laura softly say, "There's a stop sign." While I heard what she said, it didn't register that the sign was coming up fast. By the time I realized she was talking to me, my speed was way too fast for the upcoming turn. Fortunately, there were no other cars on the road when I made the sharp right turn. The occupants of the van were a bit peeved, but no one wanted to take over driving home.

#OurShade – While doing ministry as a couple, we can get tired, distracted, go too fast, and miss the signs. This is precisely where we were in our marriage. We kept missing or better yet, ignoring the signs telling us to slow down or stop some things, altogether. We must help each other stay alert and "see the stop signs," even if it means bringing everything to a screeching halt to make sure the ministry of our marriage arrives alive.

#YourShade – List all the activities you are involved in individually, as a couple, and as a family in a typical month. Use another sheet of paper if necessary. How much time does it take away from quality time in your marriage or with your family? Do you see any stop signs, such as tension or exhaustion before/after taking part in the activity, missing vital family moments, or an increasing distance in your relationship?

Activity	Time Requirement	Potential Stop Signs

35
Broke Down in Kentucky

Wayne

Laura and I were traveling to Toledo, OH in support of our Pastor. He was preaching in a week-long revival. As leaders in ministry, we wanted to ensure he had sufficient support. This could mean, ensuring his accommodations and transportation were in place, making sure any changes to the services were communicated to him ahead of time, and anything else that would make the week go smoothly. So, we packed our bags and got ready for the trip.

Laura was born and raised in Toledo, and her brother was a musician at the church we were visiting. This trip was bringing us closer to God and closer to family. It seemed like a win-win... until we crossed the state line into Kentucky.

We left North Carolina on I-40 West. Things were looking good. The scenery wasn't the most exciting, but hey, we had each other. My mind was at ease.

We drove through the rolling hills of Ashville, NC and into Tennessee. We turned north onto I-75 and crossed the Kentucky border. Things were still going smooth, despite the "check oil" light intermittently lighting up every so often. Then, our vehicle, a 1998 Dodge Durango, started to sputter. It continued to sputter increasingly until the engine sounded like every nut and bolt was about to come apart. The truck came to a stop several miles outside of Williamsburg, KY. We were stranded on the side of a dusty highway. That might not seem like much of a problem, just call for help, right? This was in 1999 and years before carrying cell phones was popular. Although we knew we were hundreds of miles away from our destination, we didn't know how far it was to the next exit. Our only option was to prepare ourselves to walk down the dusty highway to the next exit. Even though we were on a ministry assignment to support our pastor, my only concern at this point was our safety.

By God's grace, another traveler stopped and let us use his phone to call for help. Thank goodness our auto insurance had roadside assistance. They sent a tow truck, and we rode into town in the tow truck. Another example of God's wisdom and grace is that our insurance company would only cover the first thirteen miles of towing. Anything over thirteen miles would have to come out of our pocket. Can you guess how far it was from the side of the road to the only auto shop in town? Yep, thirteen miles! We arrived just as they were about to close, and they were gracious enough to keep their doors open to take our vehicle into their shop, but they would not look at the problem until the next day, which meant we had to stay overnight. At that time, Williamsburg, KY had a grand total of two hotels, and only one within walking distance of the auto repair shop, so we splurged and rented a room at a Super 8 Motel for the night. That meant we had to take our luggage out of the car and walk to the hotel. The upside was it was not raining this time, and the room was unoccupied when we arrived (see Rain Dance Romance). We found a Pizza Hut within walking distance and, unlike our first incident with a broken-down vehicle, we had a better-than-cardboard pizza!

The next day, we walked to the auto shop to talk with the mechanic. He informed us the Durango would need a whole new engine and it would take a few days to order the parts and repair our vehicle, all to the tune of $3,000! After we picked our faces up off the floor, we picked up a rental car and headed to Toledo. While on our way, we even added a delicious, historical stop in Corbin, KY, home of the original Kentucky Fried Chicken.

Laura was incredibly supportive during this whole fiasco. She never blamed me (out loud). In fact, she made sure I did not beat myself up too much for driving with the check-oil light flashing for hundreds of miles.

Side-note, we purchased cell phones as soon as we returned to North Carolina!

#OurShade – Ladies, take it from this man, in time of crisis, my wife's attitude and words (or absence of them) go a long way toward how I respond to that crisis. Husbands have the power of authority, but wives have the power to influence the atmosphere with her attitude and words. Your influence can build us up or knock us down. Luckily for me, Laura uses her power wisely.

#YourShade – It's easy to find fault with your spouse, especially if you are looking. Take some time this week to thank your spouse for things they get right, even if it's something they do on a regular basis (take out the trash, cook, clean…)

36
Missed The Bus

"The best-laid plans of mice and men do oft times go awry."
To a Mouse – Robert Burns

Laura – Somewhere around 2001, I knew Wayne was still experiencing a mental and physical rough patch. Between the many demands of work, ministry, parenting, and marriage, his ego was taking a Mike-Tyson pounding.

I was always looking for ways to encourage him, so after the kids, who by this time are teenagers, left for school, I sent him a text that read "I think you left something on at home." It didn't take a lot of thought for him to figure out what he left on and what his proper response should be. We lived less than two miles from the base, and on this day, he must have channeled his inner-NASCAR driver because he made it home in record time.

Of course, with us, there is always a "but, the rest of the story is…"

Wayne – Life happens. Amid faith, family, and career, your marriage, and your spouse can end up playing second fiddle. That's what happened to us after we moved to NC. Seymour Johnson AFB was not one of my top bases, and my career was so stagnant, I thought about retiring. The hubris of ministry had me wondering what I truly believed, and on top of all that, I lived with three teens who never nominated me for Parent of the Year. So, you can probably figure out where romance fit in the schedule.

When Laura sent me the sexy text while I was at work and I read it, I looked like Herman Munster doing his happy dance (you youngsters can Google it). I rushed home and there she is, waiting for me.

We sat on the bed, and I was in the middle of unlacing my boots when we heard a knock on the door. What!! Who could this be? The kids had all gone to school, right? Well, all except one, our son, Real. Today of all days, he missed the bus.

Please understand, he had entered the rebellious teen phase, and we weren't getting along so well, and now this. That moment gave new meaning to the term "beta blocker." So many expletives filled my mind. Fortunately, I didn't allow them to come out. Laura, on the other hand, thought it was hilarious. The look on my face nearly had her crying with laughter. I was crying on the inside, but it wasn't with laughter.

Laura – I would like to update Mr. Burns' poem to the following – "The best-laid plans are no guarantee to get you laid." The look of excitement on Wayne's face as he began to quickly unlace his combat boots (he only had time to get one unlaced) compared to the drudgery when he had to relace the same boot was amusing. Also, imagine our son's surprise when Wayne opened the bedroom door instead of me! I still laugh about this day twenty-plus years later. I am not sure Wayne has found the humor in it yet.

#OurShade – Through no fault of our own, plans may fail. It's our response that makes the difference.

#YourShade
Date Mix-up

1. Plan a date by putting each step of the date on different index cards in order (ex. step one- buy tickets to a movie, step two - get dressed…).
2. Stack the cards in order.
3. Toss the stack in the air (yes, toss it).
4. Restack the cards without looking at the correct order.
5. Carry out your date in the new order.

37
The Napkin of Doom

The napkin of doom flies across the table. Flesh collides and walls quake... is this a movie trailer? We only wish.

Laura – My father passed away in October of 2001, and our family drove to Ohio for the funeral. Dealing with our own emotional baggage of work, marriage, ministry and rebellious teenagers, our family was already on edge before we left. After traveling twelve hours with two teenagers packing foul attitudes about... well, everything, my patience reserves were getting low. Ouidii, our oldest daughter, had escaped to (I mean was in) college at the time, so she wasn't on this trip.

Everyone's emotions were running rampant, as is often the case for tragic reunions. Our family certainly is not immune to the emotional rollercoaster ride a funeral gathering brings. The whole family of brothers, sisters, moms, dads, kids, and grandbabies were gathered in my sister's small dining room. My older brother, his wife, and teenaged daughter arrived before us. When we arrived at my sister's house to meet with the rest of the family to travel to the wake together, I could tell all was not well with her crew either.

The terse words, snide comments, and veiled threats

between my adult nephews made it clear to everyone in the house these two were embroiled in brotherly animosity long before the Napkin of Doom entered the airspace. What is the Napkin of Doom? Let me explain.

A few of us tried, unsuccessfully, to de-escalate the increasing hostility. My brother, who abhors conflict, tried his best to insert some levity into the situation by cracking a few jokes. He and Wayne have a way of making people laugh and putting people at ease. They work well together, and they tried their best this day.

I was trying to act as a mediator, and as I was telling the older brother to just back down and ignore the insults, his brother threw a balled-up napkin across the table. It landed squarely (and softly) on his brother's face.

When people are hell-bent on being angry, words of peace and wisdom fall on stony ground. And these two men were hell-bent on being angry. This was proven with startling force as the two of them, each weighing over 250 pounds, jumped across the table and collided with atomic force.

Wayne and my brother acted quickly, if not foolishly, and each one of them jumped on one of the brother's backs. Mind you, Wayne is 5' 6" and, at that time, weighed under 160 pounds. My brother is 5' 9" and weighed well under 200 lbs.

Wayne – As one of the older, I mean, more mature and responsible people in the room, I felt it was my duty to help break up the fight. And since my brother-in-law jumped up and got involved, I didn't want to look as if I was scared, so I sprang into action. I should have thought of a better way to break up the fight that didn't involve me jumping onto an angry 300-pound man.

Laura -What happens next can only be described as chaos unleashed, like caged circus animals. Wayne and my brother rode my nephews like wild bulls. They charged through the dining room into the kitchen, bouncing off walls and a china cabinet along the way. I could feel the floor shaking and hear the tinkling of the glass inside of the china cabinet.

Moments before the human rodeo started, our daughter, Tasha, had just picked up an infant who'd been resting in a car seat on the living room floor. The baby was protected by my daughter and divine timing. But then I heard my nephew's wife screaming.

"My baby, my baby!"

Who is she talking about? Tasha is protecting the baby, I thought. Then I saw my nephew's tiny two-year-old son standing in the doorway between the dining room and the kitchen. He was in imminent danger of being trampled by over 700 pounds of flesh. Like a baseball player trying to dive into home base, I leaped into action and lunged into the doorway to save the tiny boy from impending doom. I almost made it out unscathed... but the 700 pounds of flesh galloping through the door captured the bun of my braided updo. The massive legs of one of the battling duo had my bun pressed against the side of the doorway. However, I'm grateful my braided bun did double duty as a cushion to protect my head, and my body had enough cushion to protect the baby from the weight forcing its way through the door!

Once the human rodeo made its way through the door and into the kitchen, Wayne, and my brother realized another child was in their path! Desperately wanting to keep her safe from harm, they deftly steered the brothers through the kitchen and towards the back door. While riding through the kitchen, they bumped into a glass table which shattered into several jagged pieces, right in front of the other child. I chalk it up to quick thinking, and divine protection that the child remained unharmed— not one bit of glass touched her.

My sister, Sharon, who was upstairs when the fight began, rushed down the steps. I don't know how she even knew something was going on downstairs. She was practically deaf, even with her hearing aids. Perhaps she felt the quaking from upstairs! She only added to the drama at this point by running into the kitchen and screaming, "Y'all broke my damn table!"

As things settled down, I saw our son, Real, crawl from under the table in the dining room, where he was "protecting" his younger teenaged cousin. It seemed like everyone was a hero, right? Except for the two who started this.

We checked everyone for injuries, and we only found a few minor cuts and scrapes, and a shoeprint stomped onto my hand. Mostly, we all were unharmed. At this point, a shell-shocked silence fell over the room. I think we all were trying to process what had just happened. A forceful knock on the door broke the silence and startled us back to reality. I jumped up and dashed to the door. It was the limo driver from the funeral home.

"Ma'am, are you all ready?"

"Ready for what?"

"To go the wake?"

Oh, yeah, the wake, that's why we were there...

"Er, uhm, can you give us a few more minutes?"

Even though the Limo could hold quite a few people, only my sister and a few of her grandbabies rode in the Limo.

When this happened, in 2001, my nephews were in their 20s. Now they are in their 40s.

I have watched them both mature as men, husbands, fathers, and yes as brothers. We recently had the opportunity to test their growth and maturity. Their mom, my sister, was in a life-or-death situation in the hospital. She was in a medically-induced coma and on life support while they had to make several extremely difficult medical decisions on her behalf.

A family meeting was called in the ICU waiting room with my sister's four children, my brother, Skip, and me. Wayne was there for moral support for all of us. I will be honest with you and admit Wayne and I had our concerns about this meeting, especially about the two who were involved in the brawl all those years ago. I was immensely proud of each of them as they discussed their mother's situation and her wishes, with calm heads and respect for each other. Even though it was a sad gathering, it was a proud auntie moment for me.

#OurShade – Sometimes we may be forced to ride out the unexpected storms of life. Our job is to hold on tight and protect the most vulnerable things.

#YourShade – What are some vulnerable areas of your relationship that need the most protection during unexpected life storms? Use the chart on the next page to discuss strategies to protect those areas and people in your family that are most vulnerable in times of storms.

Area of Vulnerability	How Can We Protect it?

38

Mr. Telephone Man

Wayne – During this time, there were few moments when Laura and I could enjoy each other without something or someone infringing on our time. Ministry, military career, and parenting consumed every moment of the day. You would think that when we had some time for intimacy, I would put everything else on hold. Well, I can't give you that satisfaction.

Once, during an intimate time, the phone rang. Without thinking, I answered the phone. Talk about a buzz-killer. The mood changed in an instant. I still don't know why I answered the phone. The only thing I can say is— that moment ranks high on the "dumbest things I've done" list.

Laura – Who was on the other end of the line? Our pastor. What did he want? He just wanted to discuss something. There was nothing urgent required. To the Pastor's defense, it was not his fault Wayne answered the phone. Your next question is probably what did Wayne do? Well, ladies and gentlemen, he put the moment with me on pause and discussed whatever the issue was with our pastor. The night was on a permanent pause with no option to rewind.

#OurShade – When we have our priorities out of order, it is a breeding ground for chaos and confusion. We will end up doing things no human or supercomputer can explain. This experience helped us to realize we had some serious work to do regarding our priorities. One major lesson was… DON'T ANSWER THE PHONE!

#YourShade - When has the inability to put your priorities in order caused you to make poor decisions that affected your relationship? What can you do to ensure the sanctity (and sanity) of your marriage is your top concern?

Activity – On a blank sheet of paper, list all your priorities as a couple. Now, on two separate sheets of paper, without discussion, each of you rank them in order of importance to you. Discuss any differences.

39
Sleeping with the Enemy

Laura – This was a turbulent time in our marriage and our family dynamics. We had allowed the demands of church ministry to overshadow our first ministry–our marriage. The amount of time we were spending together had been hit or miss for months. We spent more time together inside the church than we did inside our own home.

One night, Wayne tried to make up for it by calling me and asking me if I wanted to spend some time together (after he finished whatever he was doing at church). Although I had just put on my pajamas and settled in on the couch after a long day of driving for my job, I agreed to meet him at church. It was still early, and I did miss spending time with him, so I got dressed and headed to the church. When I arrived, there were a few other men from the congregation standing in the parking lot. For some reason, they ALL had to stop by the pastor's house for a "quick" minute. Wayne asked me if it would be okay if the other guys rode with us.

Even though I said yes, I was miffed at the thought of going over there, even for a "quick minute." I guess you might be wondering how a trip to see our pastor could go wrong, right? Let me enlighten you.

We arrived at our pastor's home, and the men got out of the car. I chose to remain in the car as a clear signal I was not in any mood to fellowship. I watched them all standing in the backyard talking and laughing. By this time in our lives, my hearing loss was more pronounced. I had become a master at reading lips and body language, even from afar. After about 15-20 minutes I saw the pastor turn toward the car in shock. I could tell by the look on his face and the tilt of his head that he didn't even know I had been in the car waiting all that time. I took a deep breath and shook my head.

Wayne and the others returned to the car. Even though it was summer, I am sure they all felt the icy atmosphere when they climbed inside the car with me. I sat silent for the entire trip back to the church, where we dropped the other men off to their own vehicles. As soon as we pulled into the parking lot, barely giving Wayne a chance to stop the car, I opened the door, jumped out and gave it a violent slam as I stormed off toward my car.

You should understand, Wayne is not a man of many rules, but one of his major rules is "never slam a door!" I purposely violated this rule, and as I did, I turned and gazed at the expressions on the other men's faces. I could only describe it as shock and awe. I mean, Wayne and Laura are the picture-perfect couple, right? I entered my own vehicle, and without a single word of goodbye, I sped off and left a car full of dazed and confused men in my departure. Ha, mission accomplished!

Once I got home, I mentally justified my behavior and prepped myself for the conversation I knew was coming. Wayne arrived, and we laid out our grievances, each of us expertly defending our own position. Although Perry Mason would have been proud, I am sure God was not pleased. We reached an impasse, neither one of us willing to back down, accept responsibility, or apologize.

Wayne decided to sleep on the couch, and I didn't bother to object.

Wayne – As I think back on those moments, I must admit it was another one of my less-than-stellar moments. I broke my promise to Laura at a critical time in our marriage. Therefore, once I realized the extent of Laura's anger, I knew it was time to show genuine remorse before things got ugly. The question for me was, "how do I show true remorse?" Apologizing was the best choice, but I let pride and stubbornness talk me out of that. The couch seemed like a reasonable choice. I thought about sleeping on my side of the bed. However, we had a full-size bed, and we had to sleep close to each other, which was not a terrible thing on a normal night. This night was not normal, therefore, if I wanted to give Laura some space, I needed to move to the couch. For that situation, I believed space and remorse were a vital part of working my way back into Laura's good graces.

Laura – This was the first time in our 14-year relationship we had slept apart due to anger. It grieved me, but not enough to offer an olive branch to fix this issue. I even considered slamming the door again on his way out, but wisdom got the better of me.

What happened next utterly pierced my heart. As I laid down, I felt a heavy presence rest upon me. I did not move and at that moment, as strange as it might seem, I could feel it enter my body. Immediately, the passage of scripture came to mind, *"Be angry, and yet do not sin; do not let the sun go down on your anger, and do not give the devil an opportunity…"*

This was a gentle and divine reminder to adjust my heart's posture, but in my unrelenting stubbornness, I just laid there, wallowing in anger, pride, and bitterness. While the love of my life laid on the couch a few steps away, I settled for sleeping with the enemy (anger, pride, and bitterness–SIN). Upon waking, I felt like a two-dollar prostitute used for the enemy's pleasure.

When the sun came up, we both decided this had to be fixed. While there were no "aha" moments of awareness for either of us, and there was still a tinge of bitterness, we both apologized for our parts and hugged each other before Wayne left for work. We still had some work to do on our relationship and our management of priorities, but this was a start.

I wish I could say things immediately got better, but I can't. They got worse before they got better. On the upside, we have not allowed anger to keep up from sleeping together since then.

#OurShade – Where do we begin with this one? Our most significant lesson was communication. I (Laura) had pent up anger and frustration about many things regarding church and priorities, so much so that I could not hold it any longer. Consistent communication is key to avoiding a crisis of epic proportions like this one was. In my anger, I deliberately disregarded my husband's wishes and disrespected him and the others who were present. I let pride and stubbornness have its way with me that night. We may not iron out all our wrinkles by sundown, but we do try to smooth them out before we go to sleep.

#YourShade – Take turns putting yourself in the position of Wayne and Laura. What would you have done differently?

40
Soul Mates

Laura – I often reflect on our assignment to Germany in 1994. It marked the beginning of our "Priscilla and Aquilla" transformation. Just like the famous couple in the Bible, we grew and served in ministry TOGETHER.

We…

…led the youth ministry- TOGETHER,

…sang on the praise team and choir- TOGETHER,

…served on the leadership committee- TOGETHER

…went on youth ministry retreats- TOGETHER!

…went home - TOGETHER.

My point? If serving in ministry doesn't bring/keep you TOGETHER then it's not TRUE ministry. You can and will serve separately sometimes, but remember, your marriage is your first ministry, and you must come back TOGETHER! We learned this lesson early in our spiritual walk while stationed in Germany and we had notable examples in many other couples in the ministry also. Sadly, we didn't always apply this lesson after we left Germany and moved to North Carolina.

When we arrived in North Carolina, we wasted no time in finding a church home and finding our respective places to serve. We were still pretty good at keeping it all together.

While in NC we lead the various dance teams organized for the church's members. That was a stretch of faith for me because I have no rhythm. I worked with the women's and girl's dance team, and Wayne worked with the men's and boy's flag team. We also were honored to perform a dance TOGETHER for a wedding. I remember dancing so hard one time my fake ponytail flew off! Even though I couldn't keep my hair together, God stretched us TOGETHER. We had some wonderful times and grew spiritually in many areas of our lives. We made some life-long friends who we still connect with on a regular basis.

Even though we had our share of pleasant memories, our time in NC was also a period of marital stress, caused by lack of prioritizing marriage and ministry. You see, amid all that togetherness, we allowed ministry outside of the home to overshadow our ministry inside of our home.

This came with a few devastating casualties. Our marriage suffered, our children were resentful of ministry and most things church. They also resented us for placing ministry demands over their needs for our time. Even though Wayne and I were often at church together, our relationship and family were silently coming apart day by day. I once considered walking away from the marriage and letting "the church" have Wayne. Of course, I reconsidered. Besides, I had nowhere to go since, I knew my family would call me crazy and send me back to Wayne, aka, the best thing in my life since sliced bread, according to my sister (See Graveyard Gratitude story). However, my point is, our picture-perfect marriage started to show a few cracks in the paint.

We managed to survive that self-inflicted assault long enough to get orders for a military reassignment to Utah. Unlike my reaction to getting orders to Germany, I was relieved. I knew I would miss my friends, but our marriage was in peril the longer we stayed. I prayed our family, our marriage, and our sanity could make it through the next six months, intact, while waiting to leave North Carolina and start fresh in Utah.

We began a slow detachment from ministry. For the first few months, we only told our pastor and his wife about our impending move. Crazy as it seems, we didn't want well-meaning people "praying against it." I recall one night after Bible Study, there was a meeting to plan the Pastor's anniversary, and the committee needed volunteers to work on flyers. That was usually my area and I always quickly responded. This night, my hand didn't go up, and everyone looked my way. The committee chairperson shot me a quizzical glance, and I looked away. After service, we called her aside and told her we had orders to Utah and would not be around much longer. Her response resonated with me, and with a sense of forlorn she said, "I bet you guys are glad, huh?"

We had never guessed other people felt the same

stresses we did, by devoting so much of ourselves to ministry. But this comment from the chairperson seemed to confirm Wayne and I weren't the only ones feeling crushed by ministry. Even those who seemed 100% "in it to win it", secretly wanted out of it. It reminded me of the ending scene in the movie *One Flew Over the Cuckoo's Nest,* when a patient breaks out of the mental asylum and the rest of the patients, while not brave enough to follow, cheered his freedom as he ran away.

The weeks leading up to our departure felt like we were licking a lemon sprinkled with sugar. Even though we focused on our sweet hopes for better days ahead, our family issues with our now adult children loomed in the background, lacing everything with a bitter flavor. However, the wheels to leave were set in motion and we would not have stopped them, even if we could.

The bitter to our lemon included our son's incarceration in another state known to be detrimental to African-American males. There was no trial date set, a terrifying circumstance for him and anguish for us as parents. We learned our daughter, Tasha, was pregnant, and once we left, she wouldn't have a place to live. Our house was on the market, but we had no buyers interested in it.

We had often told our children, "If you ever get locked up for doing wrong, don't expect us to post bail!" But it turned out we didn't have the heart to leave our son sitting in jail as we prepared to travel 2000 miles across the country. After much prayer, we decided to go against our stance concerning posting bail and, along with his mother, helped our son to be free until his trial. Our angst about leaving a pregnant Tasha was relieved when a young lady at church offered Tasha a place to stay until she got on her feet. And lastly, we had to trust God about the house and our ability to pay the mortgage until it sold. The best thing about this time was, despite the cracks in our marital armor, we were together again, not only physically, but we were also on one accord with our decisions.

Wayne will tell you, my attitude on the day of departure was drastically different than on the day we left California…

Wayne – The day of departure had finally come. We were packed and ready to go. (Notice I said we were packed, not, that I had to run around packing like in California). Before we left, I took a final walk through and around the house to make sure everything was in order.

As I was finishing the final walk through the inside, I noticed Laura was nowhere to be found. I continued the inspection on the outside and didn't see her there either. Where was she? Laura was sitting patiently in the car. This was a vast difference from the time we left California, wasn't it? This time, she was more than ready to leave. In fact, she was wondering what was taking me so long.

When I got in the car, it was like a scene from a movie.

I remember looking in the rearview mirror and sensing a feeling of relief. We made it out! This was our first military move with just us, no complaining kids in the backseat traveling with us. We could stop when and where ever we wanted to stop. Additionally, the trip would give us some much-needed time alone. No meetings, rehearsals, extra duties, and no drains on our time. Who knew a journey to Utah would be so refreshing?

#OurShade – Major change is sometimes necessary for growth. We may not always be able to change our physical location, but we can still choose to change our mental and emotional position, away from the source of whatever is causing stress in the marriage.

#YourShade – What are some things causing stress in your marriage (even if they are smaller than the issues described here)? How can you change your location to distance yourself from those stressors?

Hill AFB, Utah

2005-2009

41
Keep it All Together

"What therefore God has joined together, let no man separate."
Mark 10:9

Laura – Our next stop is Utah (we had to get a map to figure out exactly where it was) Coming from the Southern Christian-dominated Bible Belt of North Carolina and arriving in the heart of Mormon Country was a culture shock. Not only were we a religious minority, but we were also an extreme ethnic minority. Utah is less than 2% African-American. I was astonished we could travel for 10-15 minutes and never see another person of color. During our first few weeks in Utah, I would wave happily at every African-American person I saw, as if they were long-lost friends. The temporary culture shock was a small price to pay to be free from the weight of North Carolina.

Despite the culture shock, we were blessed to add to more "framily" to our lives. The first church we partnered with was in a funeral home, but they were more alive than many churches that met in fancy buildings.

Wayne – I remember the first time we drove to the church. As we turned into the cemetery, I thought, "Surely the directions are wrong." They weren't wrong. We parked and noticed we had to go in through the back. This was the same entrance/exit used to move the bodies being buried. Instead of turning around, we decided that since we came this far, we might as well go inside. As we walked in, friendly faces greeted us with genuine joy, and I haven't experienced that at every church. The congregation was small in numbers but large in spirit. It was exactly what we needed.

Laura – Pastor T. and his wife, Minister V. modeled the true meaning and joy of doing ministry together. I think it's fitting we arrived at a funeral home to revive our dying marriage! This church renewed our hope in our marriage and in each other. Watching the pastor and his wife operate out of love and respect for one another, while keeping ministry in the proper perspective, revived memories of what we learned in Germany. We were reminded that if serving in ministry doesn't bring/keep you TOGETHER then it's not TRUE ministry.

Our time with Pastor T. and Minister V. was a blessing, and when it came time for us to transition to another ministry, we remained connected with them in love.

At our new church in Utah, we found another example honoring marriage above ministry.

The First Lady Left the Church

Laura – Church can be a cruel place sometimes. You will find a mix of kind-hearted people who exude grace and love, and those who leak the oil of bitterness. This new church was no exception. The pressure and mean-spiritedness of some of the people toward the pastor's wife became so unbearable that she left to visit her mother in another state and floated the idea of never returning to the church or to Utah. She was gone for a few months! This did not sit well with Pastor Joe.

Wayne – Seeing marriages strained by ministry was nothing new. However, it didn't make it any easier to watch. We appreciated our new Pastor, Joe, and his wife, Sally. They were kind to us and accepted us as we were, not what they thought we should be.

After the prolonged absence of his wife, Pastor Joe had an announcement. He stood up and told the congregation not to make him choose between his wife and the ministry because the ministry would lose. I was with him 100%. Once again, our hope in the sanctity of marriage was renewed. It was refreshing to see people in a marriage stand up to the attack of ministry with grit and a firm commitment to each other, and effectively put ministry in its proper place. I wished I had been just as bold years ago.

Laura – I empathized with Sally. Not because I was treated poorly in the church, but because I had been at the point of walking away from the stress of ministry. I too had grown weary of the pressure of ministry and of sharing my husband with the church.

We are in a better place in our marriage now. We had to weather some honest communication about our faults and failure in North Carolina. We had to forgive each other. More importantly, and more difficult, we had to forgive ourselves.

#OurShade– We realized church service had become an idol in our marriage. We erroneously thought time spent serving in church was the same as serving God. We are not saying we should not have served in a church body. There is much honor in that labor of love. What we are saying is that our service in a brick and mortar ministry caused us to neglect our flesh and blood ministry of marriage and family, and we needed to step back and get our priorities straight. We've grown more careful of the ministry and leaders we connect our marriage with. We look for leaders and ministry partners whose priorities model marriage before ministry.

#YourShade – If you belong to a church, look at the example your ministry leaders set in their own marriage and family then ask yourself if this is what you would want for your marriage and family. If the answer is no, we encourage you to find another place to serve, together.

42
No Blanket Blues

Laura – Utah was good for us in many ways. We experienced a few firsts in Utah. We took our first cruise to the Mexican Riviera. I received my first pair of hearing aids. We also welcomed our first grandchild, Serenity, in March of 2006.

Tasha eventually followed us to Utah a few months into her pregnancy. The baby was due in March, and a Utah March was much colder than a North Carolina March. You can still see snow on the mountain tops well into May! It was freezing in the hospital room (as usual). While we were patiently awaiting our granddaughter's arrival, I was shaking because it was so cold. The nurse came in, looked at Wayne, and ever so sweetly asked him if he'd like a blanket. He accepts. Do you think she asked me if I wanted a blanket? NO!! She turned—I know she saw me—and walked out. I was thinking, "Do you spell heifer with one "f" or two?" In all fairness to Wayne, he offered me his blanket, but in my anger, I declined and CHOSE to stay angry. I was heated but still cold.

Wayne – I asked Laura if she wanted the blanket. She refused and looked at me like it was my fault she was cold. In hindsight, I should have declined the blanket in the first place and asked the nurse to give it to Laura.

But I'm not so sure it would have helped. It's like a guy going to a table full of young ladies and asking one of them to dance. If she says "No," then it's a NO for the rest of the table because you didn't ask one of them to dance with you first. In other words, sometimes, once you've messed up, there's not much you can do to fix it.

#OurShade – We shouldn't let stubbornness, anger, and pride keep our hearts cold toward each other, especially when one of us is trying to rectify a situation. It may not be anyone's fault, but it is the responsibility of both of us to come together and create a solution that works for us. We could've easily shared the blanket and in the process been closer to one another.

#YourShade – When has anger, pride, or stubbornness kept you from accepting your spouse's sincere attempt to rectify a situation?

43
Can't We All Just Get Along?

Behold, how good and how pleasant it is
For brothers to dwell together in unity!
Psalm 133:1

Wayne – Our oldest daughter, Ouidaintria (by this time she no longer wanted to be called Ouidii), was receiving her graduate degree from Western Michigan University in Kalamazoo, Michigan. Laura and I flew to Michigan from Utah with Tasha and her two-month-old daughter, Serenity, to celebrate this event. After the ceremony, we gathered in Ouidaintria's small apartment.

Let's look at the guest list: Laura, Me, Tasha, Serenity, my parents, my sister Diane, Pam (my ex-wife), and Reed (Tasha's father) and me. Reed was just stopping through to pick up Tasha and head to Toledo, but he stayed and joined the celebration with us as if he was a part of the family, even though it was his first time meeting most of the family. The beauty of the situation was everyone got along. There were no snide remarks or sarcastic jabs. We were genuinely glad to see everyone was doing well. The importance of times like that cannot be overstated. Our primary purpose was to celebrate the graduation. We ended up celebrating each other, as well.

Of course, this point where we could all get along didn't

just happen at the graduation gathering. It started years before then. We've had many occasions before, and since then, to come together in peace and celebrate our common denominators–our children and grandchildren. We have shared high school graduations, weddings, a funeral, grandbaby visits and more. Each one of us made a conscious choice to release any anger or resentment. Holding on to those feelings would have been counterproductive and physically draining. Instead of going down that low road, we took the high road. That decision ensured our children, and our children's children, would inherit and know the power of forgiveness, and the impact of genuine love for another despite any past unpleasant circumstances.

#OurShade – The pain and bitterness of the past is no match for the joy of the present and the hope for future generations. We want to leave a legacy of love for our grandchildren to flourish.

#YourShade – Are there family members you find difficult to get along with because of something in the past? What steps can you take to reach out, bridge the divide, and bring peace to strengthen future relationships?

44
No Time for Tears

Wayne – Becoming an E-9, Chief Master Sergeant, is a significant accomplishment for an enlisted military member. Only one percent of the enlisted force can achieve this rank. Reaching E-8 was challenging, and E-9 seemed out of my reach. You test for the rank once a year. If you are going to make Chief, it usually takes 3-5 years. I had reached my fifth year as an E-8 and had already tested five times. Things started looking bleak. By the time we moved to Utah, I had one chance left to make Chief. As God would have it, I finally made it. It took me so long, that I had more time as an E-8 than any other E-8 in the entire Air Force.

The ceremony for Chief is a grand event. Every part of the ceremony is well-scripted, from parking before the event, to the pictures at the end. My Daddy and my sister flew from Georgia for the celebration. The day before the ceremony, we received a phone call telling us Laura's brother, Kelvin, had died. He had suffered from health issues for some time. However, that didn't diminish the pain of knowing he was gone. Laura, being pragmatic, started planning for the trip to the funeral. While planning the trip, she didn't miss a beat in getting ready for the Chief's Induction Ceremony. In fact, Laura's actions puzzled my sister.

"Are you going to the ceremony?" Diane asked Laura.

Laura simply replied, "Yes."

Laura – That was an overwhelming day for me. I knew Kelvin was in a medically-induced coma and was on life support, but our family had hopes of recovery. I received a phone call from my oldest brother, Skip, letting me know that Kelvin's wife, with my family's full support, made the difficult decision to remove him from the ventilator. In my ignorance (or maybe it was my refusal to accept the truth) I asked would the hospital release him to go home. My brother's reply gave me a jolt of reality.

"No, baby girl, there is no going home for him after this."

It felt like my heart gained ten pounds at that moment. I asked was Kelvin able to hear conversation. My brother said perhaps and asked me if I wanted to say something to Kelvin. He said he would put the phone to Kelvin's ear so I could say goodbye. What do you say to someone existing between the borders of life and death? Between sobs, I told him I loved him, I would miss him, and I would see him again one day.

After Skip came back on the phone, I told him to keep me posted, we encouraged each other and said our good-byes. An hour later, Skip called to tell me Kelvin had passed. As the tears flowed and the memories rushed through my mind, I knew I still had my role as supportive wife to fulfill.

Wayne, of course, was comforter-in-chief for me as he also prepared to receive the military title of Chief. When his sister asked me if I was still going to the ceremony, no other answer besides yes made sense to me. As a little sister, I was hurting, but as a wife, my only desire was to support my husband. There would be time for my grief to take precedence, but at that moment, my joy for my husband was at the forefront of my mind.

Wayne – During the ceremony, Laura's smile radiated pure joy for me, and no one around us knew she was mourning on the inside. As I look back at the pictures from that night, her smile never faded. I know very few people who can get that type of news and continue to move forward without falling apart. Her decision to not let the news of her brother's death overshadow me making Chief was nothing short of inspiring.

#OurShade – When each of us is genuinely concerned about what is best for the other, both of us win.

#YourShade – What is one thing you can do to show your spouse that you place their needs above your own?

45

The Kansas Epiphany

Laura

After 30 years of military service, it was time to bid a bittersweet goodbye to the Air Force. In 2007, we had less than 18 months left in Utah and no clue where we were going to retire. We were accustomed to Uncle Sam telling us where to go. We knew we wanted to live in the south. We discussed Georgia, North Carolina, Virginia, Florida, and South Carolina, but we still weren't sure how to decide. Of course, we prayed for godly wisdom, but we still had to put some feet the prayers and make a decision.

One day, while we were driving through Kansas to visit a friend, I was looking at a map to occupy myself (boring, I know, but what else can you do when you're riding through Kansas?), and I happened to see Chattanooga, TN. Because of my severe hearing loss, Wayne and I rarely had conversations in the car. My hearing aids were no match over the noise of the car engine, wind, and traffic noises. Riding in conversational silence was the norm. I broke the silence and blurted out—

"What about Chattanooga?"

Wayne looked puzzled, mainly because the way I said it was as if we had been engaged in a conversation for a while and he somehow missed the first part of it.

"What about it?"

"We could live in Chattanooga."

My answer didn't resolve his bewilderment because neither one of us had ever been to Chattanooga, we never discussed Chattanooga, we didn't know anyone in Chattanooga, and without the map, we didn't even know where it was located. But Wayne agreed to explore the possibility. I made a mental note to research everything I could about Chattanooga when we returned home. We also wanted to seek God's guidance in our next move, so we continued to pray for wisdom and confirmation.

When we returned home an old friend of Wayne's (an ex-girlfriend actually – another long story) called to say she just retired and she now lives in… Chattanooga! Later that year, at a family reunion in Atlanta, GA, he discovered his cousin, who he hadn't seen in twenty years, lived in … Chattanooga! We took it as a sign to move forward.

After the reunion, we had planned to go to Toledo to visit my family. You must pass through Chattanooga, on I-75, to get to Toledo, so we decided to stop and spend a couple of day in Chattanooga to get a feel for the city. Wayne's friend put us in touch with her realtor, and she was gracious enough to make time to take us riding around to see different neighborhoods. She suggested some sight-seeing stops while we were there. We had our granddaughter, Serenity, with us, so we decided to try the Incline Railway. We still have the first picture we took in Chattanooga at the Incline. We had no idea we would go from being tourists to making Chattanooga our home.

We arrived in Chattanooga in June of 2009. In Chattanooga, we added more "framily" to our lives and partnered with a ministry and a Pastor and Wife team that exemplifies the beauty of marriage and ministry working together versus against each other. At The Empowerment Embassy, and under the loving leadership of Dr. David Banks and his wife, Sylvia, we both discovered our true purpose in life, and in ministry and learned how to further exemplify oneness in marriage. We are grateful for a church family that brings out the best in us and uses the gifts in us.

Even though it seemed random, I am confident Chattanooga is the God-chosen place for us!

#OurShade – Life is an adventure, and sometimes we are called to take the risk of unknown outcomes and possibilities. We embrace the moments when we don't have all the answers, trusting God to lead us in the direction He has for us. We take comfort in knowing that as long as we have each other, launching into unknown territories and experiences can be rewarding. Sometimes it doesn't matter where we end up, as long as we end up together!

#YourShade – Allow your spouse to plan a surprise date (or if you are brave a surprise trip) and refrain from asking questions about your destination. (Laura will have to work on this one!)

Chattanooga, TN

2009 - Present

46
It Has Good Bones

Wayne – After much searching, and a failed deal, we finally found a home in Chattanooga. The online pictures were less than desirable, but the square footage, bedrooms, and baths fit our requirements, so we decided to look at the house. On our way there, we passed through a nearby neighborhood that gave us concern. It didn't look like an area we would want to live in. We noticed many of the houses in the neighborhood were smaller and some sat empty in disrepair.

When we arrived, we did a quick inspection of the outside, and it was enough to pique our curiosity. We decided to ask our realtor to let us look inside. To our surprise, the house had more rooms and space than we expected. The master bedroom was spacious, and we discovered a sizeable workshop and cozy fireplace on the bottom level.

Now, the décor was another story. The house looked like it had not been updated since the 1970s. It felt as if we had time traveled back to the era of the Brady Brunch. One of the wall lamps looked like a sea-salt weathered Viking helmet, the carpet downstairs was a trampled-down shag, and every wall in the basement was covered in dark wood paneling. Looking past that, we knew a little TLC would transform this antiquated house into our home.

Laura – House hunting for me was more of an analytical process. I had a numerically weighted Excel matrix dedicated to house hunting. Whichever house had the highest score based on our wants and needs would be the perfect choice. That's reasonable, right?

This house didn't have the flash and beauty of some of the other homes we visited, but the numbers added up. Despite the dated décor, the wood-paneled walls, the disco-era carpet, and the Viking-hat wall light, this house had good bones. I could see what it could become with a few updates and a lot of TLC.

There were six bedrooms and four full bathrooms, a beautiful sunroom, plenty of cabinets in the kitchen for my culinary gadgets, and a huge backyard. Since entertaining friends and family was always a big part of our lives, I could see our friends and family enjoying this home with us.

In September 2009, this house became our home. Our joy was made even sweeter because the house appraised for $20,000 less than the asking price, so the seller had to lower the price! Of course, it needed much work! We took our time, made our list (it was an extensive one), created a budget (it was going to be expensive), and a time-frame (it was going to take a long time). We started small by repainting some of the rooms. In July of 2010, we wanted to host a gathering for both our families. The 4th of July holiday was a perfect time. We had a wonderful time, and it was delightful to see our home full of family.

Of course, there is a "but" to this story.

The day after our families left, our neighbor's tree fell on our power line, causing an electrical fire! I was upstairs on the third floor, and Wayne, Tasha (who was in her ninth month of pregnancy), Real, and Serenity, were downstairs when it happened. I recall Wayne bounding up the stairs behind the family shouting "Go, Go, everybody goooo!"

We stood outside watching the smoke and flames shoot up through the roof. The firemen arrived quickly, but they informed us they couldn't do anything until the electric company could turn off the power, which meant we had to wait, helplessly, until they arrived. With a trickle of tears streaming down my face, all I could do was pray.

"This is YOUR house, God, do what YOU want,"

As soon as the words came out my mouth, it started raining, just until the electric company arrived to turn off the power. The fire was contained, and the firemen allowed us to go in and retrieve whatever we needed. We didn't find much to salvage except a few pieces of clothing and our Bibles. The fire happened on Friday, and Wayne was on the schedule to preach on Sunday. Our family went to church smelling like smoke. What was his message that Sunday? "Things I Learned in the Fire."

We were out of our home for nearly a year while renovations were completed. The upside to the fire was everything on our to-do list was completed, at no expense to us!

We didn't even have to pay the insurance deductible, because it was our neighbor's tree and their insurance company ended up covering the entire cost. What would have taken years, and thousands of our dollars to complete, only took less than a year. We moved back in May of 2011, with an added grandchild, Harmony, who was born a few weeks after the fire.

Just as we envisioned, our home (mainly my kitchen) is filled with family and friends on many days of the week. We are the modern-day "Kool-Aid House." Many kids gather to play, and adults gather to eat, drink coffee, and share laughter. They lovingly call my kitchen, The River Café. Whenever I show the before-and-after pictures of our home, many of our friends jokingly say, "Lord, thank you for the fire!"

#OurShade – We learned to go beyond the surface to find the treasure in things that may not look picture-perfect. We trust God's process even when we don't understand.

#YourShade – Visit a thrift or antique shop and buy an item you can restore and repurpose for your home. Discuss some less than picture-perfect things in your marriage that can become a treasure with a little TLC.

47
Big Shoes & Seasoned Words

*Like apples of gold in settings of silver
is a word spoken in right circumstances.*
Proverbs 25:11

Wayne – Daddy was my hero. Our relationship was so close that he was my Best Man when Laura and I got married. He set the standard and shaped my understanding of being a husband, father, provider, and a friend. As I got older, our conversations moved from mostly monologue to dialogue, to sharing wisdom. As you can tell, I truly miss him.

In November 2010, I missed a phone call from my niece. She left a voice message saying Daddy had passed out. Daddy was 82 and still trying to do as much as he did when he was 42. I figured he was doing too much and needed to sit down. When I called back, I heard my brother wailing in the background. I asked my niece what was wrong. She informed me Daddy was in the intensive care unit in a hospital in Atlanta.

I told Laura what happened, and we drove two hours to the hospital. When we arrived, Daddy was on life support. The visual shock of plastic tubing hanging like tentacles, mixed with the rhythmic hisses and beeps of medical machinery, made it a trying time for the family. Our sturdiest pillar was now silent and immobile. A two weeks later,

Daddy died while in hospice care. I felt the weight of being the pillar transferred to my shoulders, and I told Laura I had some big shoes to fill.

"Don't walk in his shoes, make your own path," she replied.

These wise words enabled me to continue to lead forward, versus trying to go back to where we've already been.

#OurShade – A seasoned word, at the right moment, can be life-changing. Choose your words carefully in moments of crisis.

#YourShade – Since we are talking about seasoned words, find a cooking class (live or online), or try a new recipe and create a well-seasoned meal together. Discuss the impact of well-seasoned words on your marriage.

48
The Longest Ride

Laura

October 15th, 2012 began like any other typical day in the Brown house. Our daughter, LaTasha, and her oldest daughter, Serenity, were going about their routine to prepare for school. You know—finding the missing shoes, ironing the wrinkled pants, securing the homework in its folder, and other things that indicate it's business as usual. Part of that business was our daughter bringing our five-month-old grandson, Justice, into our room while she drove her daughter to school. Justice was his usual happy self, and it was always a joy to have him, even if it meant you were guaranteed to have hour-old milk vomited on you. His toothless smile was the bright spot in our day.

Tasha returned and prepared to leave for her job in the Atlanta area, taking Justice and his other sister, Harmony, with her to his dad's house. We said our usual goodbyes, Wayne always called him Sonny.

"See ya later, Sonny."

I preferred to call him Stinker.

"See ya later, Stinker."

And off they went. Fast forward to a few hours later, a family friend, Alexis, called and asked could she come by to do some work at our kitchen table. Our kitchen is the go-to place for internet and coffee. Shortly after Alexis arrived, our daughter called Wayne in distress.

"Justice is in the hospital. He's not breathing."

She called while on her way from her job to the hospital, so she had no answers to give us at that point. We asked Alexis to pick up Serenity from school (thank God for perfect timing), and we headed to the hospital which was about a two-and-a-half -hour drive.

Time seemed to be stuck like a truck in day-old mud. The traffic moved too slow for our taste, and there was nothing we could do except pray. Since I am hearing impaired and couldn't hear on the phone, I activated a few "prayer warriors" through texts and Facebook Messenger and believed for the best.

About an hour into the ride our daughter called Wayne. I studiously watched his face to discern the conversation on the other end. His downcast eyes and the way he bit his lower lip revealed the answer I did not want to hear. Our sweet, happy, healthy, and incredibly-beautiful Justice had died. The lights in my world went dark. I had no words except, "No, no, no…"

Remember, the hospital was a two-and-a-half-hour drive. We still had 90 minutes to travel down I-75 knowing our destination would end with a tragic reunion. In my defiant refusal to accept the news, I remember having the conviction of faith to believe if I could only lay my hands on him then he would arise. We arrived at the hospital emergency room and quickly went to find our daughter. She was in tears, Justice's dad was in tears, and our two-year-old granddaughter, Harmony, was in a soiled diaper. After comforting Tasha and Justice's dad, Wayne took Harmony to change her diaper. After the hugs and consoling, I asked to see Justice, ready to put every ounce of faith I owned into the miracle of raising him up from the dead. The words out the nurse's mouth fell on me like a blanket of rocks.

"They have already taken his body to the morgue."

This caused my daughter even more distress because she too had been thinking, "If only my momma can lay hands on him…" Now, I have never raised anyone from the dead before, but we both had the faith to believe I could on this day!

Even though this day turned out to be anything but ordinary, I discovered my faith was greater than I realized. That conviction of faith for the rest of our drive kept me grounded and encouraged. It kept me from falling apart like an eggless cake.

We are now living our new normal. A normal that no longer includes our sweet Justice, but it does include a new level of faith and belief in the impossible, even though we've never experienced that particular impossible.

#OurShade – Moments may come in relationships that threaten to rip the seams of sanity in two. This is when we rely on our faith to take us down roads where facts, feelings, and fear will not dare to travel.

#YourShade – What difficulties are you facing? Discuss the difference between facts, feelings, fears, and faith in relation to the crisis. How will you rely on your faith during this time?

49
Dutch Oven Casket

Who would put a dead baby in a Dutch Oven? Certainly not me, and certainly not my grandson.

Laura – The day arrived to make the final arrangements for Justice's funeral. We never thought we'd have to make such harrowing decisions. Our role was to support our daughter during this unimaginable moment in her life. We were there for physical, emotional, and financial support as she was forced to make one decision after the other. Decisions like time and location of the funeral, limo or no limo, open or closed casket were all presented with the standard professionalism from the funeral director. The next decision came at us with the impact of a freight train – choosing a casket for our Justice. How does one even go about choosing a casket for a baby? There's no way to prepare for something like that.

We went into this day vowing to let our daughter make the decisions, and even though we, along with Justice's paternal grandparents, were paying for the expenses, we were going to be silent partners. The funeral home director escorted us to the first and least expensive choice of a casket, it reminded me of a translucent jewelry box. Our daughter, knowing she had no way to pay for anything and, wanting to minimize our expenses, looked at us with red, wet eyes. I silently shook my head no (I was thinking, that's a jewelry box. I am not putting my grandson in a jewelry box.)

The next casket shown to us was a little more expensive. It was a bright white and unadorned porcelain container sitting on the floor. Once again, with those wet and sad eyes, our daughter looked at us.

"That looks like a Dutch Oven," I said, rejecting the unappealing porcelain pot as quickly as I could. "We can't put him in a Dutch Oven."

With a sigh of relief, our daughter looked at her final and most expensive option. A beautifully adorned and gracefully displayed white casket with all the frilly trimmings sitting on a pedestal with soft lighting shining upon it. The Rolls Royce of infant caskets. The choice was clear. Our sweet Justice was worth more than a flimsy jewelry box or commonplace cookware.

We knew the salesperson purposely planned the procession of choices. I am grateful we didn't have to settle for the least or be forced to go into debt to choose the best. My heart goes out to those who must make those complex decisions, under the weight of grief coupled with incurring the internal shame of a flimsy casket or the burden of an unpayable debt, to choose the best for their loved ones.

#OurShade – We are cautious when making major decisions in moments of extreme emotional distress. It helps us avoid being manipulated by emotions which could cause more problems later. We know our boundaries before a crisis occurs and remain steadfast throughout the crisis.

#YourShade – What major decisions are you facing as a couple. What steps can you take to ensure you are making wise, thoughtful decisions versus emotional decisions?

50
Great Balls of Fire

Wayne

Laura and I decided to join our daughter Tasha on a 5K Run. The run took place during the anniversary of Justice's death, and we wanted to be supportive of each other and make it a fun family run. This wasn't a regular 5K run, it was an Inflatable 5K. There were oversized inflatable obstacles throughout the course, which made the run challenging and fun at the same time

As Laura and I approached the first massive inflatable slide, which was around 20 feet high, we looked up and readied ourselves for the climb. I reached the top first and helped Laura. Next was the slide down. Laura made it down without any problems. Not so for me. As I was sliding down this 20-foot behemoth, my shorts and underwear gave me a wedgie so deep it left, uhm, let's just say…other parts exposed. Not only exposed but slapping the hot, abrasive plastic on the way down. Blap, blap, blap… blap, blap… blap. When I made it to the bottom, I tried to adjust myself without showing the pain I felt. Laura turned around as I was trying to put everything back in place.

"You okay?" she asks.

As a man, how do you respond to that question?! In a

high-pitched voice, I said, "I'm good," and we went on to conquer the remaining obstacles and finish the race.

#OurShade – There will be obstacles along the marriage journey. A firm foundation and strong support are crucial to finishing the race intact. We always remember, even though we are both going through the same situations, we are two different people (physically and emotionally), and we may experience it differently. We make sure to check on each other, regularly. A simple "are you OK?" goes a long way to help finish the race with courage and grace.

#YourShade
Obstacle Course Challenge
- Find an obstacle course race you can participate in together (use wisdom, based on your level of fitness).
- Have an obstacle course party in your yard or a park and invite other couples to join you.
- Plan a laser tag date with other couples. Play on the same team as your spouse then play on the opposing team. Discuss the difference.

51
Dream Team

The Wind Beneath My Wings- Bette Midler

Wayne – I grew up in a home where my father was the sole provider. He was the head of the house. We attended a male-dominated church, and the woman was viewed as the weaker vessel. Therefore, my idea of manhood meant I should shoulder the responsibility for making sure my family had everything they needed. I still hold this as a core belief (somewhat).

As time went on, my experiences with women would reshape my thinking. Dating was a most confusing process. Some women wanted me to take the lead, while others wanted me to move over and hang on for the ride. One of my dating relationships ended in marriage, and the marriage died in divorce. I must admit, my faulty perception of men's and women's roles played a part in the demise of my marriage. Thank God for His grace in giving me a second chance.

One of the many lessons I've learned is each woman is an individual God has created with purpose and potential. My role is to cultivate these qualities through continuous support. This means I am TEAM LAURA all the way. I am the team's manager, sponsor, and most passionate cheerleader. In this role, I am not a Chief Master Sergeant, CEO, or center of attention. My support may be simple as being a sounding board or server of her favorite tea.

My words were put to the test when Laura had an idea about writing a book. I must admit I had no clue how much that process entailed. However, that didn't matter. My first questions were, "What do you need?" "When do you need it?", and "Where do you want me to put it when I get it?" As head cheerleader, I wanted her to know I was all in.

As a result of Laura starting a book camp in 2014, over 60 people have fulfilled a lifelong dream of writing a book. Those books have inspired and transformed others exponentially. I sometimes think about the day she came to me with the idea. What kind of negative impact would I have made if I was stuck on stupid and tried to discourage her from going after her dream? Thankfully I don't need to dwell on that question. The question I have now is, "What's next?"

Laura – I also grew up in a house where dad was the provider. I also watched my mom take on jobs to make sure he knew she could contribute too (when she felt like it). When I was twelve, my mom died of cancer, which left my dad to figure out his new role as a single parent. I was the last child; my siblings were grown and had families of their own. Daddy went to work, cooked, cleaned, went to parent-teacher meetings, and doled out wisdom. One of his most memorable pieces of wisdom was, "No man likes a woman with her hands always out." That meant I needed to bring something to the table in a relationship.

When Wayne and I got married, I was also active duty in the Air Force, so bringing something to the table was easy. Once my enlistment was over, finding something to bring to the table was more difficult because I equated that with something monetary. I came to understand Wayne didn't need my financial contribution as much as he desired my support in what he wanted to achieve in his military career.

In the Air Force, making Chief Master Sergeant is the epitome for an enlisted person. It would take dedication and sacrifice from the service member and his family. It meant, if a move would increase his chances for promotion, I gave up whatever job I had and moved. Even if I was close to finishing a degree, I stopped and moved. Other than my initial response to moving to Germany, I gladly sacrificed my wants to ensure he could take advantage of any opportunity to advance. Seeing him put on those Chief stripes so proudly made it all worthwhile!

Now that Wayne is retired, we both had to find another focus. We discovered our individual purpose and our marriage purpose and began to pursue things related to each. There are times when I support his vision, and there are times when he supports mine, such as when I created the S.W.A.T. Book Publishing Camp. Even when our visions are seemingly separate, we stay together in our commitment to support one another. We have learned to be comfortable in our roles as leaders–whether that means one of us is the visionary leader for a project, and the other is the support leader. We flow into our ever-changing roles with joy and excitement.

I tell everyone Wayne is my biggest fan and loudest cheerleader, and they see it in action also. I savor my opportunities to cheer him in his endeavors also. With all this cheering going on, we are a definition of marriage out loud!

#OurShade – Success, sacrifice, and unwavering support should never be one-sided. Both of us need opportunities to grow. It has taken time, but we've learned how to best support and encourage each other, and how to allow ourselves to be supported and encouraged. We relish each role: as the player, coach, or the number-one fan who cheers throughout the game, from beginning to end.

#YourShade – Discuss with your spouse what each role, visionary leader (the one with the idea), or support leader (the one helping to bring the vision to reality), looks like to you, and what you need from each other in those roles.

51 ½
The 1/2 Has Not Been Told

We're in This Love Together – Al Jarreau

As we celebrate our marriage, we look back and smile at the memories made. There are many more than 51 ½, and some stories ended up on the cutting room floor. We have had our highs and lows, some laughter, and tears. We've had gains and losses, but the most important thing is, we did it TOGETHER, and we are still in this love together.

We are often asked how we knew that the other person was "the one."

My (Wayne) answer was I realized I could really be myself around Laura. I could be funny, sensitive, insecure, and vulnerable without judgment. There wasn't a *specific* moment in time, but, there were those *special* moments that let me know she was the one.

My (Laura) answer is always the same, "Whenever I thought about and pictured my future, Wayne was always there... in every scene... we were in this life TOGETHER." I thank God daily that it wasn't just my imagination... my dream came true.

We are still making "shades," so our story is never complete!

The Sum of All Shades

1. Embrace and value your authentic self.
2. Silence your inner critic and engage in honest communication with your spouse.
3. Laugh at yourself.
4. Stay untangled from deceit.
5. Lead with confidence versus ego.
6. Focus on hidden treasures.
7. Learn to let go of some things.
8. Learn to recognize the signs of unchecked baggage.
9. Don't project your fears and worries onto your spouse.
10. Decide to move forward and don't look back.
11. Find joy in moments that go awry.
12. Learn the best way to encourage your spouse.
13. Always protect each other.
14. Don't miss opportune moments waiting for the perfect time.
15. Learn the art of sacrifice.
16. Be careful who you invite into your marriage.

17. View your spouse with fresh eyes.

18. Have brave conversations.

19. Practice silence and let God speak to your spouse.

20. Learn to conquer sexual temptation.

21. Be a source of pride versus embarrassment for your spouse.

22. Fidelity is the best choice, not the only choice. Choose wisely.

23. Make family decisions with wisdom and unity.

24. Know your "peacekeeping" plan in times of crisis.

25. What you resist may be the thing you need the most.

26. Don't get comfortable after a success.

27. All communication is not effective.

28. Other people may need more of your spouse's attention than you.

29. Learn to give and receive sincere tough love.

30. It's not the size of the "BUTS" that matter, it's how you handle them.

31. Don't let others force their dreams and desires on your relationship goals.

32. Technology is not a replacement for reality.

33. Adjust to accommodate your spouse's changing needs.

34. Don't go too fast and miss the signs.

35. Men have the power of authority, women have the power of influence. Use your power wisely.

36. Plans may fail. It's your response that makes the difference.

37. Protect the most vulnerable things in times of calamity.

38. Lack of priorities is a breeding ground for chaos and confusion.

39. Consistent communication is key to avoiding a crisis.

40. Major change is sometimes necessary for growth.

41. Choose marriage models wisely.

42. Don't let stubbornness, anger, and pride keep your heart cold toward your spouse.

43. The pain and bitterness of the past is no match for the joy of the present.

44. Be concerned about what is best for the other person.

45. Trust God to lead you in the direction He has for you.

46. Go beyond the surface to find the treasure in the small things.

47. A seasoned word, at the right moment, can be life-changing.

48. Rely on your faith versus facts, feelings, and fear.

49. Avoid making major decisions in moments of emotional distress.

50. Both of you may experience the same situation differently. A little understanding goes a long way.

51. Success, sacrifice, and unwavering support should never be one-sided in a marriage.

> *We would love to hear your thoughts and suggestions about 51 ½ Shades of Brown. Please consider leaving us a review on Amazon!*

Meet Wayne and Laura

Wayne is an author, mentor, professional speaker, and community leader in Chattanooga. He is a 30-year US Air Force veteran. Wayne has a Bachelor of Science and a Bachelor of Biblical Studies degree. He is the author of "Listen –Wisdom and Wit for the Next Generation." Wayne is a native of Albany, GA (pronounced "All-Benny").

Laura is an author, speaker, and workshop facilitator. She is the owner of the Serious Writers' Accountability Training (S.W.A.T.) Camp where she helps aspiring authors create literary legacies and unleash their inner superhero through writing. She created Wells of Truth Peer-Based Bible Coaching Group, where she teaches students how to study the Bible by using diverse study techniques. Laura is a native of Toledo, Ohio.

Wayne and Laura are certified marriage coaches and certified Purpose Discovery Specialists. They have three children and two grandchildren and enjoy planning "Pop Pop & Nanna Surprise Adventures" for their granddaughters.

Other Publications

Wit and wisdom packaged in bite-sized anecdotes

A weekly bible study & creative art journal for Psalm 119

A collection of poetry by local artists

Images to color while you meditate on the beauty of God's word in Psalm 119

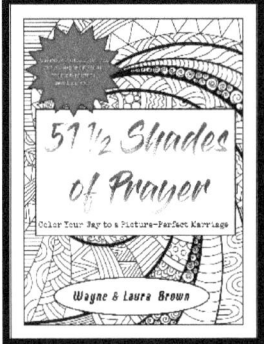

Pictures and scriptures to color your way to a vibrant marriage

A collection of Self-reflection questions

Workshops & Coaching Events

Picture-Perfect Power Couple Marriage Encounter

*A two-day event designed to empower couples with creative strategies to cultivate a satisfying and productive marriage

Dream Team – Power Couples Unite!
- o   Discover Your Purpose
- o   Develop Personality Synergy
- o   Learn Your Lead Language

Picture This – The Power of a Vision-Driven Marriage
- o   Discover Your Marital Purpose
- o   Develop Your Marriage Vision Statement
- o   Design Your Vision Canvas

The Art of War - Handle Conflict with P.O.I.S.E. & C.A.L.M.
- o   Practice Communication Etiquette
- o   Discover D.A.M. Barriers to Listening
- o   Master the Weapons of War

Get S.H.I.F.T. Done – The Power Couple System for Success
- o   Develop a plan for your next Power Move
- o   Create S.U.P.E.R. S.M.A.R.T. Goals
- o   Design Your Next Level

*Ask about the virtual Picture-Perfect Marriage Encounter